JOHN
WAYNE

THE GENUINE ARTICLE

JOHN WAYNE

THE GENUINE ARTICLE

★ ★ ★

The Unseen Archive
of an American Legend

MICHAEL GOLDMAN

foreword by
PRESIDENT JIMMY CARTER

preface by
ETHAN WAYNE

INSIGHT EDITIONS

San Rafael, California

CONTENTS

THE LOYAL OPPOSITION

AMONG THE MOST MEANINGFUL OF THOUSANDS OF CONGRATULATORY TELEGRAMS I received in November 1976 upon winning election to serve my country as the thirty-ninth president of the United States was a simple note from John Wayne that read, "Congratulations sir from one of the loyal opposition." I had been a voracious consumer of John Wayne movies and an unabashed fan dating back to my youth. Even upon becoming president, I was thrilled to receive good wishes from such an important figure, as anyone else would be.

I did not know him personally at the time, and I was under no illusions that his political sensibilities would always align with mine—he had, in fact, supported my opponent, President Gerald Ford, and he would go on to express disagreement with me on a host of issues in the coming years. But what quickly became apparent to me as my term in office got underway was the fact that when John Wayne called himself the "loyal" opposition, he meant it. He graciously agreed to participate in my Inaugural Concert, and he always promoted the notion that the nation had but one president—a distinction that trumps, it seems to me, party loyalty or ideological disagreements. During my time in office, his correspondence, notes, suggestions, and criticisms sent my way were always respectful and heartfelt—offered up because he believed what he was saying was in the nation's best interests.

Then, in 1977, as discussed later in this book, he boldly decided to risk friendships and the image millions of people had of him as a stereotypical conservative icon to become among the highest profile and most vocal supporters of my drive to get the US Senate to ratify the Treaty Concerning the Permanent Neutrality and Operation of the Panama Canal and the related Panama Canal Treaty. He did so because he felt it was the right thing to do and for no other reason. He lobbied Republican senators—some among his closest friends—to vote for ratification, and in the end, our position prevailed. To this day, I believe both the American people and the people of Panama owe John Wayne a debt of gratitude for taking such a stand late in his life when he was certainly under no obligation to do so.

As he fell ill, I stayed in touch with his family and representatives and monitored with a heavy heart his deteriorating condition. A few weeks before we lost him, in time for his final, seventy-second birthday, I was pleased to sign into law bill S. 631, ordering that a specially designed gold medal be struck in John Wayne's honor out of gratitude for his innumerable contributions to our nation. Upon signing the bill, I declared that, "for nearly half a century, Duke has symbolized the American ideals of integrity, courage, patriotism, and strength and has represented to the world many of the deepest values that this Nation respects. His conduct off the screen has been as exemplary as that of the characters he has portrayed. He has served, and will continue to serve, as a model for America's young people."

I was pleased and honored to visit Duke during his final stay in the hospital, and I was thrilled that he asked other members of his family to join us for introductions and photographs. When he passed away on June 11, 1979, I joined millions of John Wayne fans around the world in mourning the loss of a legendary performer and, more importantly, a truly great American. I'm proud that I had the opportunity to eulogize John Wayne's passing and honor his life on behalf of the American people in my role as the nation's chief executive.

"John Wayne was bigger than life," I told the nation shortly after his passing. "In an age of few heroes, he was the genuine article. But he was more than a hero. He was a symbol of so

PAGES 4–5: *On the water: a lifelong lover of the outdoors (see Chapter Eight).*
OPPOSITE: *A pensive John Wayne, late in life. He remained involved in national affairs until his death (see Chapter Six).*

many of the qualities that made America great. The ruggedness, the tough independence, the sense of personal courage—on and off the screen—reflected the best of our national character."

Like John Wayne, I meant every word of what I said on both of those occasions. What I learned from him as we engaged during my tenure as president was that patriotism, policy debates, even major disagreements about the nation's direction need not be hostile or personal or contentious, and that no matter how much we disagreed, we had more in common than our differences might suggest. In today's turbulent national climate, with so much of the debate over what is best for the nation poisoned by personal attacks and rigid ideological orthodoxy—translating into gridlock in Washington, DC—it's a good lesson to remember and emulate. John Wayne frequently disagreed with me—in fact, he didn't even vote for me. And yet, I considered him a supporter, and I was certainly an unabashed fan of his.

We need more of that kind of interaction in our dialogue today. We need more John Waynes.

—PRESIDENT JIMMY CARTER, AUGUST 2012

TOP: *John Wayne's copy of the Mailgram he sent President Jimmy Carter congratulating him on his election. Wayne used the phrase "loyal opposition" in messages acknowledging the electoral victories of three Democratic presidents—Kennedy, Johnson, and Carter.* OPPOSITE: *Classic John Wayne pose late in life—as President Carter called him, "The Genuine Article."*

NORMAL GUY, EXTRAORDINARY LIFE

I DON'T REMEMBER ALL THE DETAILS, but when I was nine years old, my father, John Wayne, brought me to the New Mexico location of the movie he was filming at the time, *The Cowboys*. I visited the set of the film for the duration of my Easter vacation in 1971. When the week was up, my dad made the decision to let me stay with him a few extra days. He notified my school in Costa Mesa, California, that I'd be missing the next week of school, and then he explained to the late journalist Wayne Warga—who was also on location as part of his ongoing attempt to collaborate with my father on a book about his life—why he did so. Warga jotted a note with Wayne's answer on it, but it took three decades for my dad's reasoning to finally make its way to me.

For more than thirty years, since John Wayne's death in June 1979, that note sat unread and unnoticed along with thousands of other documents to and from, by, about, connected to, or describing my father during his life. Indeed, the vast majority of my father's personal papers of all types simply sat in boxes for years. One of those papers was Warga's note explaining why I was kept from school after I had just finished vacation—just one of the many nuggets that journalist Michael Goldman, working with John Wayne Enterprises, found as we researched this book.

John Wayne—then sixty-four, still working, not in the best of health, and raising his second family, including me, his third and youngest son—explained himself in a way that touched me to the core when I finally read it, three decades later.

"[Ethan's] nine and I want to be with him," my dad told Warga. "He'll be fourteen before I know it and something happens. They start to drift away and they don't come back until they're thirty. At thirty, they realize what fatherhood is. My oldest boys are in their thirties now and they've come back. But with Ethan, I won't be there when he's thirty, so I've got to love him now."

He was right—he was gone long before I was thirty. I was seventeen when he died, in fact. But his words from so long ago

remind me how lucky I was to get seventeen years—some people aren't so lucky. In this case, I don't mean the actor or icon "John Wayne." I mean my dad—a normal guy who led an extraordinary life.

In those seventeen years, I was fortunate to have dozens of experiences like that stay in New Mexico. My father brought me along whenever he could. When he went on location without me, though, I was pretty miserable. I'd ask him when he'd be back, and he'd say, "In about three months, God willing and the river don't rise."

I hated it when he said that, but fortunately, I frequently got to his locations for extended visits—school or no school. I enjoyed all sorts of adventures across this country and the world—in Europe, Mexico, Canada, and on our boat, the *Wild Goose*, during those seventeen years.

By the time he decided to give me a small role in the movie *Big Jake* in late 1970, just ahead of making *The Cowboys*, it was no big deal—just another exciting thing to do. I wasn't thinking about acting—I was thinking, "I get to stay

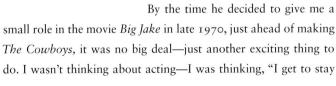

OPPOSITE: *On the set of* El Dorado *in 1966.* INSET: *For the last seventeen years of his life, John Wayne's regular companion was his youngest son, Ethan Wayne, whom he frequently took on set with him.*

in Mexico longer!" I was just a kid having fun. They said, "Act scared," and I would act scared. The stuntmen were my friends; so were the technical guys, the wranglers, the cook, the cast members. It was like a traveling carnival—there was the strongman over there, and over here was the fat lady—all these colorful characters. I had a lot of freedom, with access to horses and motorcycles, and got to visit exciting new places and meet unusual and interesting people. It was priceless.

My dad made all that possible simply because he wanted to spend time with his kid. That's the kind of *person* he was. Myself; my siblings; my mother, Pilar; and a handful of close friends knew that *person*. The rest of the world, to this day, knows the icon.

So, when we finally opened up the John Wayne archive a couple of years ago to see what was stored there for so long, we realized that we had uncovered within the thousands of documents in those boxes the story of John Wayne the *person*. So we prepared the groundwork for this book—the first opportunity

ever in print form to talk about the man using his own words from his own letters and other papers.

Numerous books have been written about my father—some well intentioned, by those who spent a bit of time in his life or admired him; some just to make a quick buck by connecting to his name; some by family members; and some that are serious academic studies of his film work. The better ones are meticulously researched biographies by scholars, and these occasionally feature my dad's voice through archival interviews from over the years. But none of them has ever allowed John Wayne to speak for himself, offering his perspective.

RIGHT: *Ethan Wayne's fondest memories from his youngest days involve adventures with his father, such as fishing trips to Mexico.* TOP: *With his dad at their Newport Beach home.* OPPOSITE: *A young Ethan gets some handgun lessons from his father on the set of* The Cowboys.

13

14

"FOR MYSELF, I ALREADY KNEW JOHN WAYNE WAS A GREAT DAD, BUT SOME OF THE MATERIAL WE FOUND GIVES ME A FAR GREATER UNDERSTANDING OF WHAT A COMPLEX AND FASCINATING MAN HE WAS ON A PERSONAL LEVEL."

—ETHAN WAYNE

What we found in the archive was John Wayne doing just that—speaking for himself about the fun, the joys, the work, the pressure, and the pain. It's all in those boxes.

My father pulled a heavy cart—he worked until near his death, largely because he had to. So many people—millions—wanted a part of him in so many ways. There were bills to pay, contracts to fulfill, employees to support, people to help, businesses to run.

Great joys are preserved in those boxes as well: traveling the world, escaping out to sea on the *Wild Goose*, forming deep bonds with some of Hollywood's great pioneers and most interesting characters, raising his family, running a huge household with my mother, speaking his mind on national affairs when he felt compelled to do so, and dealing with the unending onslaught of fans, business associates, and others who wanted, in some way, to connect with John Wayne.

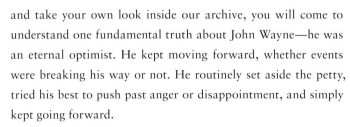

It's all in those boxes.

Therefore, John Wayne Enterprises decided to finally open them up, and with Michael Goldman bring you in this volume a personal and inside look at my father's life in a way that has never been presented, or even conceived of, until now.

For myself, I already knew John Wayne was a great dad, but some of the material we found gives me a far greater understanding of what a complex and fascinating man he was on a personal level. You may or may not have liked all his movies, agreed with his politics, or even thought much about what it must be like to be a common man living such a public life. But as you dive into the pages that follow,

and take your own look inside our archive, you will come to understand one fundamental truth about John Wayne—he was an eternal optimist. He kept moving forward, whether events were breaking his way or not. He routinely set aside the petty, tried his best to push past anger or disappointment, and simply kept going forward.

When I was young, I used to race motorcycles. My dad never particularly liked me doing it, but he let me pursue my interests. At one point, I kept running over a rock on the course. I told my dad that I stared at the rock in order to avoid hitting it, and I hit it anyway—over and over again. That, he taught me, was precisely the problem.

"Only look where you want to go, son," he said. "Never look where you don't want to go. Because wherever you look, that is where you are going."

The same is true in life.

The documents in the John Wayne archive, taken cumulatively and in context, make a strong case for that philosophy, and they confirm that is precisely how my father lived his life. He made conscious choices about how to live, and he never took his eyes off the places he wanted to go. That, in turn, made him the person I knew and loved as my father—a positive, kind, uplifting, and optimistic man who always tried his best and taught me more lessons than I could possibly count—some still unlearned.

I'm pleased to be able to share that real and fascinating person with readers of this book. In today's particularly complex and fast-paced world, where any of us can lose our way through the frenzy and pressure of daily life, John Wayne's wit, wisdom, humility, and decency are particularly instructive. We found that wisdom throughout the contents of the John Wayne archive. Now, in the pages that follow, you can discover it for yourself.

—ETHAN WAYNE, AUGUST 2012

OPPOSITE: *Today, Ethan Wayne readily concedes he idolized and tried to emulate his famous father, as he did here as a young boy on the set of* The War Wagon *in 1967.* INSET: *John and Ethan Wayne during one of their periodic trips to either British Columbia or Alaska onboard the* Wild Goose.

THE GENUINE ARTICLE

EVEN IN 1966, AFTER DECADES OF STARDOM, John Wayne felt he wasn't interesting enough to have people examine or care about his personal life, opinions, or correspondence. Officials at the University of Oregon felt differently. In December of that year, they wrote to him, hoping to procure Wayne's papers as the basis of a special "John Wayne Collection" at the university library.

"I am most complimented by your suggestion to set up a 'John Wayne Collection,' but I'm afraid that at the present time my files are too meager to be of any interest as a collection," Wayne wrote back. "Thank you for your thoughtful interest, but in regard to your request, I think you should write to me again in ten or twelve years."

It didn't take nearly that long for others to push Wayne to tell his personal story. Starting in 1969, journalist Wayne Warga repeatedly attempted to get Wayne to commit to writing his memoirs. After penning an article for the *Los Angeles Times* about the making of Wayne's movie *The Undefeated*, Warga began promoting the book idea relentlessly.

Wayne was lukewarm, at best, to the concept. Even while thanking Warga by letter for the *Los Angeles Times* article, he pushed aside the notion.

"I can only tell you in advance that my only interest in a book about me starts with my retirement, which is so far in the offing as you can see on a clear day," Wayne wrote Warga on May 2, 1969. "Seriously, I would like to put down some reminisces of the past forty years in my business—but in the future… way in the future."

Warga kept pushing, enlisting West Coast literary representative Charles B. Bloch that same year to let Wayne know publishers were, in fact, interested. Wayne put them off, saying he was too busy for the next year and a half anyway, but maybe "after that, I might be interested."

Bloch and Warga tried again in early 1970, with Warga pleading with Wayne in a letter to "consider a book." On January 27, 1970, Wayne wrote back giving general, grudging approval to the concept, quoting a famous line from Charles Dickens's *David Copperfield*, saying that, if they could go slow and easy on it, "Barkis is willing."

About two years later, Wayne finally brought Warga around to spend time with him while he was making *The Cowboys* in New Mexico in 1971; later, Warga spent three weeks with him on a fishing trip to Canada on Wayne's boat, the *Wild Goose*. Over time, they wrote fragments of Wayne's early story, calling the embryonic manuscript *What Hat, Which Door, and When Do I Come In?* But eventually, John Wayne backed away. In a 1982 proposal for a never-written book titled *Barkis Is Willing*, about his relationship with Wayne, Warga said Wayne told him he wanted to wait because the biography "needs a better ending."

Warga wrote that Wayne said, "Hell, it's over with [third wife] Pilar. It's getting harder and harder to get pictures made. I just don't know. I want a different ending."

This concern over how to finish his story, when Wayne himself saw no end in sight, permeates the correspondence discussing a biography. John Wayne seemed to see no relaxed retirement on the horizon to serve as a platform from which to look back on his rich life and relate stories from the optimistic perch where he felt most comfortable. In fact, by 1976, the last time Warga saw Wayne on the set of *The Shootist*, the ending, from Wayne's personal point of view, remained beside the point. He was still pushing forward, not looking back.

OPPOSITE: *John Wayne appreciated family time most of all. Here, he clowns with his grown sons Patrick (left) and Michael (right) and their kids, with daughter Aissa on his shoulders, among other family members. Behind Wayne is his brother, Robert Morrison.*

"I REMEMBER THE PLEASANT AND HUMOROUS THINGS, NOT THE TRAGEDIES. I THANK GOD
THE HUMAN MIND HAS LITTLE MEMORY FOR PAIN AND I THANK GOD I HAVE VIRTUALLY
NONE AT ALL. THERE IS PAIN IN THIS BOOK, AND I HAVE KNOWN TRAGEDY. THERE IS
ALSO ANGER. BUT MOST OF ALL, THERE IS CELEBRATION."

—JOHN WAYNE, FROM HIS UNFINISHED AUTOBIOGRAPHY

More than thirty-five years have passed since then, and John Wayne has been gone more than thirty years. He left behind reams of personal letters, telegrams, speeches, handwritten notes, annotated scripts, interviews, news clippings, and commentary, not to mention the memories of those who knew him intimately. Today, this book presents a look at Wayne's life through the prism of those intimate documents, photos, and memories—many of which have never been seen nor shared before. In addition to material from the John Wayne archive, this volume includes additional Wayne Warga material on John Wayne from Warga's personal papers, located at the Edward L. Doheny Jr. Memorial Library at the University of Southern California; additional letters between John Wayne and his friend John Ford, from the Lilly Library at the University of Indiana; and intimate Wayne family

and friend interviews conducted by the author over the course of 2012. These remarkable assets, along with rare photos and images of Wayne's possessions, offer excellent insight into the legendary actor's perspective on the joys, trials, and tribulations of his life, as well as a rich and complete look inside Wayne's personal world.

It's a unique story. Wayne labored hard to maintain a normal life under the abnormal, pulsating glare of international fame. John Wayne was a big movie star, no doubt, but he was also a father, a husband, a confidante, an employer, a world traveler, a businessman, a man of strong beliefs and loud tone, and usually an optimist, always ready for a joke or a spirited debate.

Above all, the documents in the Wayne archive reveal that John Wayne was truly a sensitive soul. He genuinely cared about people, his country, his kids, and his legion of fans, often telling his children not to complain when family outings were interrupted by overzealous fans because fans "gave me a career" and "they pay the bills." In fact, with the support of his thirty-five-year personal secretary and close friend, Mary St. John, Wayne built an entire infrastructure around the notion that his fans deserved to hear from him, and so he replied to them religiously, as this volume illustrates in Chapter Seven.

"Get the idea of running away out of your mind," he lectured a young woman named Jane Davidson of South Dakota in a November 11, 1969, letter. Davidson had written to Wayne asking for a picture and casually mentioning she was scheming to leave home. The actor cautioned, "The older you get the more you'll realize that you can't run away from your problems, whatever they are—and that running away will never bring you happiness."

Perhaps most illustrative of John Wayne's true nature was the relentless normalcy of the man. As a young actor, he was quite aware he was not a natural talent, that he came to acting from being a crewmember—a "regular guy"—and he never forgot that person. Some of the strongest memories his youngest son, Ethan Wayne, has about his dad, in fact, revolve around mundane things like not wasting water when taking a shower on board the *Wild Goose* or the best way to push a broom.

"As a kid, I had to sweep these things that came off a big rubber tree in our front yard every day," Ethan Wayne recalls. "He'd come out and say, 'That is not how you sweep. You sweep like this.' So, to this day, when I sweep something, I still think about him teaching me to sweep the proper way with a big push broom."

Wayne's daughter Melinda Wayne Munoz emphasizes that the Wayne children were expected to get good report cards, frequently rode the bus to school, and had to save money for things they wanted, just like anyone else. The surviving Wayne children, in fact, say that despite the unusual nature of their father's fame, it was not until they became teenagers that they fully grasped that their lives were not typical and that their father wasn't exactly like other dads.

Ethan Wayne says it finally dawned on him something was different in his life while accompanying a friend to the friend's mailbox. The friend pulled just a couple letters out of their mailbox, and Ethan recalls wondering, "That's all the mail you get? Getting the mail at our house was a dreaded chore for an eight-year-old carrying in large mail cartons full of letters and packages."

Confidantes and family members admit Wayne could be quick to anger, but he was also quick to cool off, to forgive and forget what he was angry about in the first place. No matter how difficult things got, at the end of the day, John Wayne would find a note of optimism somewhere in the situation and the energy to push past the difficulties. That was true even as he engaged in his final battle with cancer, according to his oldest surviving son, Patrick Wayne.

"Most of the time that he was lying in that hospital dying of stomach cancer, he gave me the impression he really thought he could beat it, that maybe the doctors didn't know what they were talking about—he was mostly upbeat when we were around," Patrick remembers. "He was talking to us, trying to make us feel better, give us some hope. He knew what was going to happen, and yet, in spite of that, in his mind, he maintained an upbeat attitude for his family."

As the documents in the Wayne archive show, that attitude permeated Wayne's life. This volume offers context and examples in John Wayne's own words. However, this book makes no pretense of offering up the full biography—that is readily available elsewhere. Nor do all the memories presented here always match perfectly with how these stories have been told in other places over the years. This book presents, simply, the way John Wayne and those around him saw, felt, and talked about things at particular key moments in his life.

It's a story that offers a valuable lesson for students of the human condition. That lesson is that a single individual, even one constantly spotlighted under the bright glare of fame, can privately, personally, and deeply influence those around him in a way that far outshines even his impact as a global figure. By telling Wayne's story this way, it's hoped that more people will come to understand the real man behind the icon in all his many layers of complexity.

So with that said, please turn the page, step inside the Wayne archive, and personally meet John Wayne, the genuine article. ✪

OPPOSITE: *Jovial John Wayne.* INSET: *Wayne with his wife, Pilar, at their Newport Beach home.* PAGES 20–21: *John Wayne as rancher Wil Andersen in 1972's The Cowboys.*

CHAPTER ONE

ROOTS

"It was a job and not much else at the time.
A job was important enough. The big depression
was still two years away, but my one personal
depression was staring at me from the bottom of my
empty soup bowl. I needed a job."

—JOHN WAYNE, FROM HIS UNFINISHED AUTOBIOGRAPHY

THE STARK REALITY OF MEAGER PROSPECTS IS WHY, according to John Wayne, Marion Mitchell Morrison of Glendale, California—a student and football player at the University of Southern California—eagerly grabbed an opportunity to work in a relatively menial job as a prop man at Fox Studios in the mid-1920s. Wayne's version of how he came to work at a movie studio for the first time, as related in his unfinished autobiography with Wayne Warga from the early 1970s, makes it all sound so pedestrian—he was a young man looking for work.

In the biography, Wayne wrote that he was still on scholarship with the USC football team, but nonetheless hurting for cash, when he got his first part-time job as a prop man, thanks to an assist from silent cowboy acting legend Tom Mix. At the time, Mix helped USC football players as part of a strategy for procuring football tickets (see page 29).

Wayne's manuscript never mentions the famed bodysurfing accident that reportedly injured him and led to the loss of his football scholarship, according to numerous sources. He states simply that "I knew I had cast my lot with the film industry," and so "I quit school mid-way through my junior year and went to work full-time as a prop man at Fox."

However, Wayne did declare repeatedly over the years that he lost his scholarship, which required him to find employment to survive during turbulent economic times. In his 1973 speech to the National Football Foundation and Hall of Fame, for instance, he stated it was his leg that was injured, playing football when "a gentlemanly opponent broke my leg for me." He declared himself "thankful" because "if it hadn't been for football and the fact I got my leg broke and had to go into the movies to eat, why who knows [what would have become of him]?"

In any case, whatever the details are regarding the injury that terminated his football scholarship, it's clear that, upon losing that financial support, Wayne simply thought things over,

"HE NEVER TOOK ANYTHING FOR GRANTED. HIS LIFE WAS BASED ON HARD WORK
AND PREPARATION AND MORE PREPARATION AND HARD WORK."

—PATRICK WAYNE

decided what was best, and took his chances, come what may. He clearly saw old-fashioned work as a better ticket for covering food and essentials at that point in his life. Although he couldn't know it at the time, that pragmatic decision was the start of Wayne's transformation into a major national figure.

Indeed, taking risks and banking everything on his ability to excel through basic hard work were Wayne's hallmarks before and after he became famous. They were traits Marion Morrison developed at an early age, long before he got to USC, and ones he never abandoned.

"If you gave him an opportunity, he took advantage of it," his son Patrick Wayne explains. "He would develop it and work on it. He never took anything for granted. His life was based on hard work and preparation and more preparation and hard work. He never stopped learning or being curious, and he was always trying to improve himself."

He already had a stubborn independent streak by the time his family left Winterset, Iowa, for Glendale. Morrison was just four by then and already being called "Duke," after a family dog, by just about everyone who knew him. As he grew older, he was routinely tasked with looking after his younger brother, Robert, upon whom his feisty mother, Molly, doted. Indeed, Molly took Marion's original middle name, Robert, and handed it over to his new brother as his first name when he was born.

During those formative years, young Duke also watched his father, Clyde, struggle financially in a series of failed ventures, as his parents' marriage slowly unraveled. They would eventually divorce in 1930.

Such life experiences certainly must have fed his inclination to be his own man and do his own thing. But Patrick Wayne suggests his father developed that independent streak by internalizing a healthy dose of his mother's—pardon the expression—true grit as part of the recipe for his eventual success.

"His mother was always the driving model for his will to succeed," suggests Patrick Wayne today. "They might have been dirt poor, eating Saltine crackers and peanut butter for lunch, but my grandmother always had him in a clean shirt and shoes. She was connected politically [locally] and worked on campaigns and things, and was a real go-getter. So, from early on, he saw he should want to succeed. He excelled in

---

PAGE 22: *Entering his teen years, Marion Morrison in his Sunday best growing up in Glendale, California.* OPPOSITE, TOP: *The Morrison family in Glendale (left to right, Marion, Robert, Molly, Clyde). The Airedale Terrier pictured is the dog Duke, from whom John Wayne got his nickname.* OPPOSITE, INSET: *Youthful portraits of Mary Brown (later Mary, or Molly, Morrison) and Clyde Morrison, John Wayne's parents.* BELOW, LEFT TO RIGHT: *The toddler Marion Morrison already playing cowboys and Indians; Molly Morrison with her sons Robert (center) and Marion; brothers Marion (left) and Robert Morrison as youngsters. Marion frequently cared for his brother, at their mother's behest.*

SENIOR DANCE

Marion Morrison
Chairman.

sports and scholarship in high school, actively wanted a further education, and only went to USC because the family had no political connections to get him into the Naval Academy. If he had stayed in school, I don't doubt he would have gotten into politics—he had that kind of drive. But, as fate would have it, he lost his scholarship and didn't have the education, and he simply had to get a job. So he became a prop man, got some experience in the summers, and that made it natural for him to think he could leave school and do well in that field if he could just get in through the door."

Indeed, Marion Morrison was already a high achiever before he got to USC, if his 1925 high school yearbook, the Glendale Union High School Stylus, from his senior year is any indication. A tour through it clearly illustrates that Marion

---

TOP LEFT: Images out of Marion Morrison's 1925 high school senior yearbook indicating his participation on the football team and in running the senior dance. RIGHT: One of his many USC hats. Wayne was devoted to USC his entire life, despite leaving during his junior year. OPPOSITE: A famous, classic gridiron pose of Marion Morrison, the USC football player.

Morrison was a thoroughly accomplished student by the time he graduated.

He was president of his senior class, after having served as junior class representative and vice president of the junior class the year before. He played varsity football, was senior dance chairman, student chairman of the reception committee, on the stage crew, was a student assistant in "cafeteria management," a participant in the Southern California Shakespearian Contest, served as a sportswriter on the school newspaper, served on the senior ring committee, and earned an honor pin, among other accomplishments.

At USC, despite not graduating, he began a lifelong relationship with his brothers in the Sigma Chi fraternity, and he established a connection with the football program and university that continued until the end of his life. He routinely attended events and ball games at the school and was a member of just about every alumni organization that existed, as well as a regular donor to a number of causes at USC. Thus, the university awarded him an honorary doctorate in fine arts in 1968, and his bust is now on display in Heritage Hall on the USC campus.

Such unbroken connections over decades are indicative of another signature quality that typified the man—loyalty. Once he liked a person, a place, or a thing, he maintained his allegiance, come what may. Such loyalty and unyielding constance with those he loved, respected, and trusted resulted in many lifelong friendships and associations, but it also periodically led to business associations gone wrong and personal disappointments as well. Nevertheless, loyalty was a trait that first surfaced in his earliest years and that never left him.

For instance, in 1930, after Wayne's parents divorced, his father, Clyde, remarried almost immediately to a woman named Florence Buck, who already had a daughter, Nancy. Eventually, Wayne bonded with his stepsister, who later became Nancy Marshall, and with his stepmother, and he played an important role in their lives. As gracious letters from Nancy Marshall to John Wayne indicate, he quietly provided financial support for his stepmother's medical bills in her declining years, and he gave

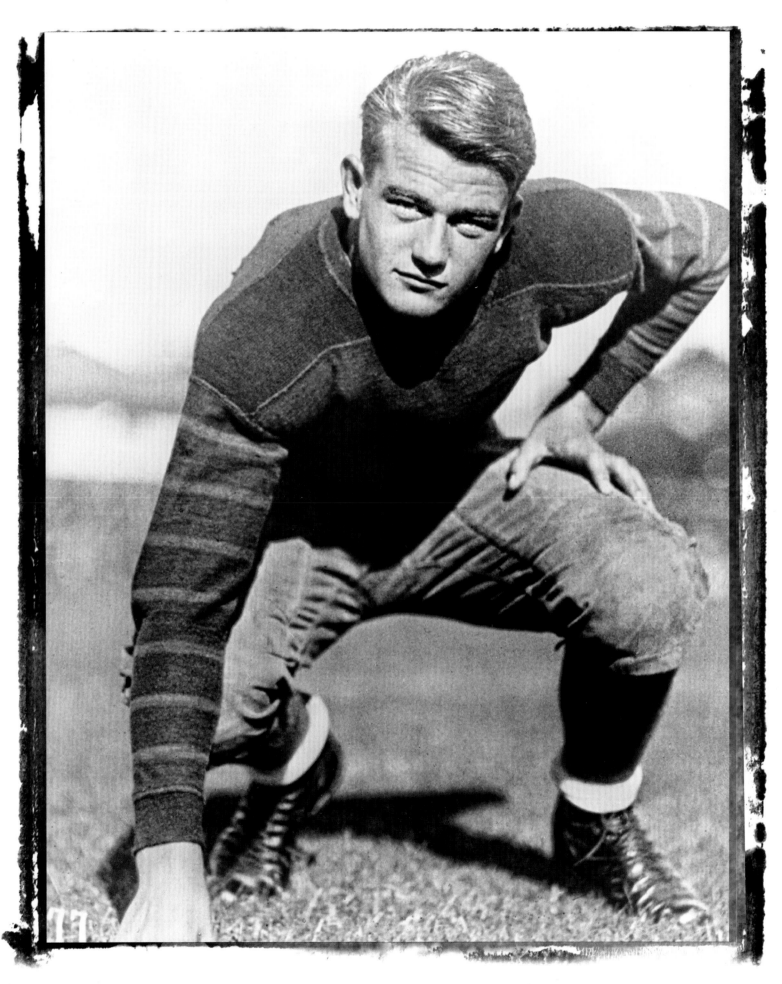

Nancy Marshall occasional work reading and evaluating novels—commonly called "coverage" in the industry—for possible motion picture consideration. There is no evidence that her work led to any of Wayne's eventual pictures, but Wayne's actions reflect his abiding sense of basic loyalty.

Remarkably, it appears that Wayne told almost no one outside of his loyal secretary, Mary St. John, who periodically corresponded with Marshall on Wayne's behalf, that he was assisting that side of his family in any way. In fact, his surviving children today say they knew nothing about it; they barely even knew Florence and Nancy.

And yet, on August 4, 1974, Nancy Marshall quietly wrote John Wayne to inform him her mother had passed away in Oklahoma. The deeply emotional letter profoundly thanked her stepbrother for his help and told him how much he and his father had meant to her and her mother:

> *You have been so kind through the years and we have been truthful in saying we don't know what we would have done without your help. Without the money you have sent for so many years, my mother could not have had the extra medical care she has required. I am intensely proud of John Wayne, but love and respect Marion Morrison. Your father taught me so many of my values and replaced my own father, who never cared about children. Please write me soon when you have the time. I know you are a very busy man but I need to hear from you occasionally and know first hand that you are well and happy.*
>
> *Much love, Nancy*

The combination of Wayne's work ethic and loyalty would pay off almost immediately after he left school to labor on dusty soundstages at Fox. The Depression was preparing to wash over America, but Wayne had managed to situate himself within the one industry that would manage to find a comfortable niche during that uncertain era—the motion picture business.

There, he would shortly make a lifelong friend who would help him start down a path no one could possibly have predicted for the handsome son of a struggling drugstore clerk with a funny name. ✪

TOP LEFT: *A teenage Marion Morrison with Josephine Alicia Saenz during a Palm Springs outing. He was just 19 years old and she 16 when they met. They later married, and she became mother to his first four children.* LEFT: *Marion Morrison posing in a football uniform during his high school years.*

The irony is profound—almost ninety years ago, the man who would go on to become the most iconic cinematic cowboy in history was busy racking himself with worry over how to make an impression on ... the most iconic cinematic cowboy in history. At least that was Tom Mix's reputation in the fall of 1927 when Marion Morrison encountered him.

The young USC football player and one of his pals were sent by football coach Howard Jones to meet Mix one day with a promise that Mix could help them find part-time work that might, if things worked out right, lead to bigger and better things.

"What had me excited was the prospect of becoming a sparring partner for Mix who just happened to be my hero," John Wayne reminisced in his unfinished autobiography. "Mix, we were told, was such [a] tireless boxer, that he needed two of us to get a good workout. A classmate, Don Williams, and I made the trip to Hollywood and the busy Fox studio. All the way there, we tried to figure out how to make the best impression possible on the greatest cowboy star in the world."

Instead, Mix made an impression on them, Wayne wrote, once they met him on the Fox lot near "his big limousine with 'T.M.' stamped and embossed on what looked like all 10 doors. We walked into his suite of dressing rooms and there he was, all done up in his fancy cowboy clothes."

When it came time to go a few rounds, Morrison and Williams were surprised to find out Mix only wanted them to watch him box with a regular sparring partner. He then filled their ears with promises of crew jobs on location in Colorado, where he would

John Wayne's boxing pose. He liked to work out and box, and his athletic background played a role in his introductions to both Tom Mix and, later, John Ford.

soon be heading to start on a new picture, *The Great K & A Train Robbery*.

As Wayne wrote, Mix said, "I know you boys want to get in condition so you can come up there with me and we'll run and you'll train with me and we'll all be in great shape."

Then, Mix asked Morrison to line up across from him and "show me how to play football." Wayne claimed he went into a football crouch and allowed Mix to "push, pull, and tug at me" in order to determine "just how tough a football player was."

The movie star eventually declared the tussle "interesting," casually mentioned "it would be a while before I go to Colorado," and so he offered to "see what I can find for you in the meantime." He introduced them to "the man in charge of getting jobs at Fox," and Mix promptly left. Marion Morrison shortly found himself "on the swing gang in the Property Department, and my job was carrying furniture from one set to the next."

His second day on the job, Wayne claimed in the manuscript, Mix drove by in "his beautiful locomobile."

"I quickly put the chair down and smiled at my benefactor. 'Hello, Mr. Mix.'"

He received "a blank look" in return—a look "that told me my date with Colorado had just been broken. He didn't remember."

Biographers suggest Morrison did work briefly on Mix's picture in Colorado, although his own manuscript implies otherwise. In any case, Tom Mix's mentorship was short-lived. But John Wayne stayed on in the prop department and soon found a more meaningful mentor.

CHAPTER TWO

DETOUR
INTO
ACTING

"I DECIDED TO BECOME A DIRECTOR, AND IF NEED BE,
I WOULD TAKE A BRIEF DETOUR INTO ACTING OR WHATEVER
ELSE WAS NECESSARY TO ACCOMPLISH MY GOAL."

—JOHN WAYNE, FROM HIS UNFINISHED AUTOBIOGRAPHY

Supposedly, it started because, once again, someone thought it would be interesting to test Marion Morrison's mettle as a football player. At least, that's how Wayne describes his first interaction with the man who would become his mentor—director John Ford. In 1926, according to what John Wayne wrote in his unfinished autobiography manuscript, he was assigned to "herd geese" on the set of a Ford film when the animals would stray from their designated area. Wayne wrote that Ford casually remarked, "I hear you play football," and "after a short exchange of words, I assumed my position waiting for push, pull and tug. But it didn't happen." Or, not in the way that Morrison was expecting.

"Ford, sporting a mischievous grin, started to crouch down too. He kicked my arms out from under me and sent me sprawling face down on the rough plaster. Everyone laughed and applauded. Ford looked pleased. I didn't take too kindly to this so I got up and said, 'Let's give her another try.'"

Wayne wrote that, this time around, when Ford tried to run past him, he kicked out his left foot, meaning to trip the legendary director, and instead knocked him in the chest. Suddenly, "Ford was splattered in his own plaster mud on his own backside."

It's hard to know if events transpired precisely that way—some Wayne biographies describe this incident a bit differently, and some a lot differently. Wayne's rough manuscript was obviously written in his voice and from his point of view, describing events the way he wanted them to be perceived. However, beyond his embryonic manuscript, there is no other firsthand written account from John Wayne himself about his early days as a prop man at Fox, even in the Wayne archive. That document abruptly terminates as *Stagecoach* makes a splash in 1939; sometimes it matches interviews he gave journalists over the years, sometimes it deviates, and sometimes it treads into territory he had never publicly discussed before.

In any case, it's clear this incident launched Wayne and John Ford down the path of a close friendship. In the document, Wayne wrote that Ford laughed at the confrontation and that the incident earned Wayne acceptance. "From then on, it was 'Hello, Duke.' I was one of them," he wrote. "I began to realize these were the kind of people I wanted to be around."

Morrison hadn't officially quit school yet, but eventually, the Ford relationship led to him propping more or less full-time. During this period, he got kicked off Ford's set once or twice for various indiscretions, including inadvertently stepping in front of a camera. Down the road, though, he was asked to stand in as an extra in front of the camera in the movie *Hangman's House*. Morrison had already been used fleetingly as an extra in crowd scenes in a couple of other films, but this was the first time he would be recognizably visible, even though the part required him to do little more than stand in "the prisoner's box" as "the condemned man" before returning to his propping duties.

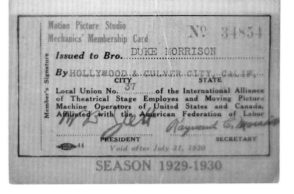

Ford grew fonder of Morrison, and he kept the young man on his prop crew and began using him more as an extra. One time, in fact, in 1929 for the movie *Salute*, Ford not only gave him his first on-camera speaking role, but he paid Morrison to recruit former USC football players to appear in the film and mother-hen

them on the train ride across the country from LA to Annapolis, Maryland. On that train ride, Morrison met and began a lifelong friendship with a fellow USC student. According to Wayne in his unfinished autobiography, the train was getting ready to leave Los Angeles, and "the last player to arrive, an hour late, a dollar short, one pocket torn and a gin bottle hanging out of the other, was Ward Bond." Bond, of course, would go on to become a leading character actor in Hollywood and one of John Wayne's closest chums until Bond's untimely death in 1960 (see page 132).

Following *Salute*, Morrison found himself getting semiregular work as an extra or stuntman at Fox, thanks in no small measure to John Ford.

"By 1930, I had dropped my [propman's] hammer and appeared—often briefly—in seven films," he wrote. But during this period, he emphasized, "I had no thoughts of becoming an actor. Acting to me was a kind of apprenticeship toward becoming a director. It was also a source of petty cash. I wanted to direct. I was dead-set on becoming a director."

And so, Morrison began strategically studying John Ford.

"In the years to come, Ford would teach me everything I know about filmmaking," he wrote. "The feeling I would come to have for scenes and just about anything else would come from standing behind him and watching him work. The strength of his craftsmanship—more than craftsmanship—his special sort of genius attracted me. I also had enormous respect for his ability and following my disastrous experience on *Hangman's House* [when Wayne spoke without permission and was severely reprimanded by Ford], I watched everything he did."

Wayne referred to this apprenticeship period as his "detour into acting." It was a detour that lasted until his death—he would ultimately direct just four films.

Wayne does not elaborate in the manuscript on why he never made directing a priority in subsequent years. As his writing illustrates, opportunities were abundant in the film industry in those early years, particularly for someone with a resourceful nature who was willing to work hard—Morrison was a useful guy to have around.

As he wrote, labor rules were particularly loose in Hollywood back then, and "it was possible for the enterprising man to move from propping to juicing [electrical work] to acting to doubling, and then back again. I occasionally worked as a stuntman."

PAGE 30: *A young John Wayne eventually rose from being a prop man to stunt work to working as an extra to speaking parts to B movie roles during his early days in show business. His handsome looks no doubt helped this trajectory.* OPPOSITE: *Marion Morrison relaxes in 1928, just before ending his college career to join the workforce.* INSET TOP: *John Wayne's original union card, made out to "Duke Morrison," when he started working at the studios as a prop man.* INSET BOTTOM: *His Stuntmen's Association honorary card. Wayne had worked formally and informally as a stuntman and helped pioneer movie fighting techniques over the years, thus earning the honor.*

In developing his on-screen identity, John Wayne was, more than anything, a sponge—he picked up things from everyone he worked with. According to his unpublished autobiography, during his early days churning out quickie Westerns, no one was more essential to his cinematic education than "some good stuntmen."

The first he named was Tom Bay, a stuntman and actor who Wayne referred to as "one of the toughest men I ever met." The next two influences, he wrote, were stuntmen Allen Pomeroy and Eddie Parker. On several films directed by Robert Bradbury, "We worked out a new system of fighting," Wayne wrote. Pomeroy and Parker "also helped in this new way to throw punches. There were no direct blows and no one got bruised. It was easily twice as effective and realistic. One of the fighters would stand with either his back or side to the camera and I'd swing. I'd throw a punch past his jaw and off past the side of the camera. My opponent would jerk his head and reel back as I was completing the swing. Through the camera, it looked as though I had connected square on his jaw. But because of the angle no actual contact was needed; just the need for the other fellow to react as though he was really hit on the jaw or wherever we had decided to aim the punch. This way you could take a full-out punch without hurting your opponent. It revolutionized the stunt fighting game."

Next, Wayne credited Yakima Canutt, a legend in the stunt world who is best known for, among other things, the famed stagecoach horse-riding stunt in *Stagecoach*. Wayne wrote about befriending Canutt and becoming close collaborators. Canutt was, in addition to his movie work, an award-winning rodeo champion and cowboy, and Wayne spent countless hours observing and learning his techniques for horse riding, roping, using guns, fighting, and more.

Meanwhile, many of Wayne's acting mannerisms were copied from or taught to him by famed actor Harry Carey Sr. and

character actor Paul Fix. During the 1920s, Carey had been a major silent film star and had worked closely with John Ford. Ford had a young Wayne study Carey's work; later, Wayne worked with Carey directly, and they became great friends. Fix is credited with helping Wayne develop his so-called rolling gait walking style; Fix did so after Wayne told him he was uncomfortable with how he walked on the big screen.

"He learned from all of them," his son Patrick says today. "His mentor for a long time was Harry Carey Sr. He idolized [Carey], and certainly the way he carried himself was based on watching Harry Carey. With Yakima Canutt, they developed modern-day screen fighting, horse action, and things like that. My dad was very young then, and he was a big guy, but he was very catlike. He could move like the wind and had that incredible work ethic. Also, his balance was incredible. He could handle a horse as well as any stuntman at the time."

OPPOSITE, TOP: *John Wayne with friends Montie Montana (center) and Harry Carey Sr. Both appeared in his movies—Montana was a rodeo star and stuntman, and Carey was a silent film star, after whom Wayne patterned many of his famed Western mannerisms.* OPPOSITE, BOTTOM: *B cowboy film star John Wayne engages in one of dozens of stunt fights. During this period, he helped develop many on-screen fighting techniques.* TOP: *John Wayne (top row, fifth from left) joins a group of Western movie luminaries for a group photo at an industry event.* CENTER: *A signed picture to Wayne from his friend, stunt legend Yakima Canutt, who is in the picture.* BOTTOM: *In* Paradise Canyon *with Yakima Canutt in 1935.*

As a result, Morrison was used as an extra, stuntman, and in tiny speaking roles in seven pictures in 1929 and 1930, while helping out wherever else he could along the way. Then, one day in 1930, what has come to be known as his big break finally happened. Ford pointed Morrison out to another famous director, Raoul Walsh, who decided to give him a screen test for an upcoming project, *The Big Trail*. That legendary screen test has been dissected many times—how he was tested without sound, with sound, was forced to work with a dialogue coach, and how the filmmakers deliberately tried to trip him up during the test, among other things.

What's clear from Wayne's own account is that, despite his inexperience and the curveballs intentionally thrown at him by other actors, he largely won the day with gumption. For instance, when another actor peppered him with questions out

of a script Morrison had not read, he wrote that he had previously "paused to think of answers to every other question, but this time I became the aggressor. I referred to [the other actor's] pale hands, white clothes and gallant charm as being of no value on the trail."

TOP: *John Wayne in 1930's* The Big Trail, *his first starring role.* RIGHT: *A publicity event for* The Big Trail. OPPOSITE: *The famed picture of the young Wayne launching his quest for stardom during the film's marketing campaign.*

DETOUR INTO ACTING

Because of that bold, improvisational approach, "I got the job," he declared.

Next, Marion Morrison got a new name—John Wayne (see page 40)—and then, "two weeks later, I was starring in my first film, a leading man with virtually no experience. I would serve my apprenticeship as an actor later. Would I ever! My salary was $75 a week—no small amount of money in those days—at least not to me. The Depression was in full swing. I was hooked—and secure."

Wayne was just twenty-two years old at the time. *The Big Trail* hardly launched his career into orbit as he had hoped; the movie proved to be a box-office disappointment. Yet with it, the Hollywood apprenticeship of the newly minted "John Wayne" had begun. Among other things, it involved learning how the press operated. He wrote about feeling awkward going on a publicity tour for *The Big Trail*. At first, studio honchos billed him as "a football player turned actor," and later as a "cowboy turned actor." But on a publicity swing through New York, his picture appeared in the *New York Daily News* with an arrow pointing to his brand-new Bulova wristwatch, blowing a big hole in the story that he was some kind of real cowboy.

"That was my first collision with the press," he wrote in his biography manuscript. "It certainly wouldn't be my last."

Still, Wayne's performance earned him a seventy-five-dollar-a-week contract at Fox, and so he joined Hollywood's B-movie assembly line. In his next role, he was miscast in a movie about a male basketball player going up against girls in *Girls Demand Excitement* (1931). During that film's press tour, he was promoted as an All-American member of USC's national championship football team. That, he wrote, "drove me into a state of fury," since, of course, he had left USC and had nothing to do with winning any championship.

"It was a total misrepresentation and I raised hell, but a lot of good that did—the story had gone out. I was sure I'd never live it down," he stated in his manuscript.

All of which caused the young actor to start, in his words, "sulking" on the Fox lot one day, bad-mouthing the studio, the film, and himself. At that exact moment, he claimed, none other than famed humorist Will Rogers walked by and asked him what the matter was. Wayne wrote that after patiently listening to his litany of complaints, Rogers said, with irony in the shadow of the Great Depression, "You're working, aren't ya?" When Wayne replied that was true, Rogers told him to "keep it up" and strolled away.

"I've never forgotten that advice. It hasn't hurt," he wrote.

For close to a decade, Wayne found himself churning out one-reel Westerns at a frenetic pace—what he called "quickie Westerns." Wayne's career didn't advance much during this period, but there was lots of bonding, drinking, carousing, and making lifelong friends. It was, Wayne wrote, a period in which "fights, falls, stunts in five- and six-day Westerns filled my summers. Hunting and fishing in Mexico filled my winters."

During filming season on the quickies, the work was back-breaking, with little reward beyond learning the movie business. He wrote that "the longest hours and hardest work was in those years. One day I staggered home after working 26 straight hours."

Some of it, he added, "was crazy," like the time they tried to turn him into a singing cowboy known as Singin' Sandy or sometimes Singing Sam.

"The biggest problem was that I couldn't sing," he recalled in his manuscript. "Then, they got a fellow [who could sing] and another to play the guitar. They stood on either side of the camera, while I sat in front of it mouthing the words and phony-strumming a guitar."

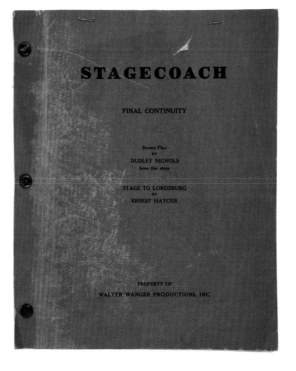

Wayne gamely played along for a few pictures until, on a publicity tour one day, he rode a horse onto a stage, only to be embarrassed when his horse relieved himself while the audience yelled for Wayne to sing. He wrote that he soon stormed the office of Herb Yates, president of Republic Pictures, and insisted the farce come to an end. That, he claimed, is what led Yates to hire Gene Autry to fill the niche of "singing cowboy" a few years later.

"John Wayne never sang again. Count your blessings," he declared in his unfinished autobiography.

Nevertheless, John Wayne really learned his craft during this period—how to dress, stage fight, handle weapons, ride a horse, and all the rest. He also worked with a handful of people who became highly influential on the development of his on-screen style. In particular, he met and absorbed everything he could from cowboy actor Harry Carey Sr., character actor Paul Fix, and legendary stuntman Yakima Canutt, among others (see page 34–35).

Finally, in 1938, Ford rather casually asked Wayne to offer suggestions for a new picture he was developing based on the Ernest Haycox short story "Stage to Lordsburg." For the lead role of Ringo Kid, Wayne suggested Lloyd Nolan, an actor whose recent performance he had enjoyed in *The Texas Rangers*. Wayne biographies suggest the discussion lasted a couple of days on board Ford's boat, *Araner*, during a cruise to Catalina, but in his manuscript, Wayne wraps it up in a couple of lines.

"Hell, Duke, can't you play it?" Ford apparently asked Wayne, who wrote: "I said yes and spent the next two years worrying Jack [Ford] would see Lloyd Nolan in [*The Texas Rangers*]."

Wayne also claimed it was actually his idea to shoot the film in Monument Valley, on the Utah-Arizona border, but that he good-naturedly accepted it when Ford announced a couple weeks later that he, Ford, had discovered Monument Valley as "the perfect place to shoot a western picture."

"So far as I'm concerned," Wayne added, "John Ford discovered Monument Valley. I guess you might say I found it for him to discover."

In any case, Wayne, now thirty, suddenly and quite unexpectedly found himself graduating from the "B" team. From the first previews, *Stagecoach* was a hit. No one was more surprised than John Wayne.

"I had never in my life seen anything as exciting as the [first] preview [in Westwood, California]," he wrote in wonderment. "The way those kids took to the picture was tremendous. They laughed, clapped, stomped, and obviously loved it.

"At an age when most leading men are starting down the wrong side of the hill, I became a star." ✪

OPPOSITE, TOP: *Early headshots taken of Marion Morrison when he was launching his acting career.* OPPOSITE, BOTTOM: *A movie poster for one of his early Westerns, the 1934 film,* Blue Steel. INSET: *The cover of Wayne's copy of the* Stagecoach *script.*

Wayne almost never answered to plain "John," however, and remained "Duke" to family, friends, and fans alike. His legal name remained Marion Mitchell Morrison—it was never officially changed. Periodically, when doing business or applying for passports, he would have to produce his original birth records to prove it. For some reason, near the end of 1972, he started collecting his birth documents. He wrote to the County of Los Angeles asking them to officially "certify" that he was, in fact, born "Marion Robert Morrison" and to send a copy of his original birth certificate, stating that "I have used the name of John Wayne for the past 43 years, both in my business and professional life." About a month later, in January 1973, he wrote to the clerk of birth records in Winterset, Iowa, requesting an additional three copies of his original birth record.

"wrestled" with the name he was then using—Marion Michael Morrison. In and of itself, this name was surprising, since his legal name was Marion Mitchell Morrison. Wayne had been born Marion Robert Morrison, of course, only to have his mother legally change his middle name to Mitchell. Wayne, however, never thought much of "Mitchell." Some time in the late 1920s, according to several biographies, when studio publicity material mistakenly started calling him Marion Michael Morrison, he decided it fit better and started using it professionally.

In any case, Sheehan didn't like the Morrison variations. Walsh supposedly suggested Anthony Wayne, but Sheehan worried that was too ethnic, and so he casually chose "John Wayne." The name stuck, with little opposition from the man in question.

"I was determined to be as cooperative as possible," he wrote. "After all, Fox had given me a great many opportunities, first as a prop man and then as a stuntman and an actor. They had started what was called a star build-up campaign for me. Who was I to complain? Sheehan, an imposing, business-like man, wanted something that sounded very American. He said my name would be John Wayne. John Wayne it was."

To this day, even within the Wayne family, the legality of the name remains murky. His son Patrick, now seventy-three, says his own name was never legally changed—technically, on official records, he remains Patrick John Morrison. All the children from Wayne's first marriage were born with the surname Morrison. The children from his third marriage, on the other hand, were born with the name Wayne.

ABOVE: *A selection of John Wayne's passports from over the years.* OPPOSITE: *A 1948 affadavit required to enter Mexico, explaining his name situation and signed twice—as Marion Morrison and as John Wayne. Note distinctive signatures for both names, both of which he had to use on official documents throughout his life.*

"My passport would say 'Morrison AKA Wayne' for years, but after so many years, I just go by my married name, Melinda Wayne Munoz," his daughter Melinda explains today. "But my birth certificate says Melinda Ann Morrison. And where my father signed it, he wrote 'Marion Morrison, AKA John Wayne.'"

"Obviously, we are Waynes," Patrick says, settling the matter with a smile.

NEW YORK, N.Y.
A D M I T T E D
FEB 8 1962

IM. & NATZ. SERVICE
NEW YORK, N.Y. 106
A D M I T T E D
OCT 3 1963

CLASS

4

Renewal, extensions, amendments, limitations, and restrictions

THIS PASSPORT IS NOT VALID FOR TRAVEL TO OR IN COMMUNIST CONTROLLED PORTIONS OF

CHINA
KOREA
VIET-NAM

OR TO OR IN

ALBANIA

IMM. & NATZ. SERVICE
NEW YORK, N. Y. 96
A D M I T T E D
OCT 31 1960

CLASS

IMM. & NATZ. SERVICE
NEW YORK, N. Y. 107
A D M I T T E D
APR 3 1963

CLASS
TO

AFFIDAVIT IN LIEU OF PASSPORT

This is to certify that I, Marion Mitchell Morrison, known as John Wayne, am a United States Citizen, born May 26,1907, in Winterset, Iowa.

My present residence address is 4735 Tyrone, Van Nuys, Los Angeles County, California.

Marion M Morrison

John Wayne

Subscribed and Sworn to before me this

4ᵗʰ day of March 19 48

Beatrice Benjamin

Notary Public in and for the County of Los Angeles, State of California

BEATRICE BENJAMIN

My Commission Expires November 25, 1991

VISA NUMERO 254

**CONSULADO GENERAL DE MEXICO
EN LOS ANGELES, CALIFORNIA.
BUENA PARA DIRIGIRSE A MEXICO**

VALIDA POR NO-INMIGRANTE - 6 meses

DERECHOS: PESOS: GRATIS DLS

A PARTIR DE MAR 5 1948

P. O. DEL CONSUL GENERAL
EL CONSUL

GUILLERMO LOPEZ ZAMORA

Esta visa no es suficiente para ser admitido de Mexico, pues los inmigrantes deberán, además, sujetarse al examen de las autoridades de Migración y Sanidad, las que en definitiva resolverán sobre el particular.

CHAPTER THREE

WESTERN MAN

"THE PROSE, POETRY, AND SONGS THAT HAVE BEEN WRITTEN
ABOUT THE WEST FAR EXCEED ANY OTHER NATION'S LEGENDS.
I GUESS MORE IS SAID ABOUT THE COWBOY THAN ANY
OTHER NATION'S HEROES. THE COWBOY APPEALS TO
A BASIC EMOTION—HEROIC TRADITION."

—JOHN WAYNE, FROM HIS UNFINISHED AUTOBIOGRAPHY

JUST SIXTEEN MONTHS BEFORE HIS DEATH, John Wayne found himself particularly excited about the prospect of getting a brand-new, handmade Western-style gun belt and holster from legendary gun leather craftsman John Bianchi. On February 22, 1978, Wayne received the belt and holster, and according to a letter he sent Bianchi, "immediately whipped it on and found the belt fit perfectly."

Wayne, however, never shy, remarked that since Bianchi asked for his suggestions, he was happy to offer a few. Over the years, he had developed a specific way he liked to wear a gun, and so he asked Bianchi to make some revisions.

"In order to make it handy to get a gun out, I have always used a reinforced leather on the front of my holster," he wrote to Bianchi. "Carry the holster over the gun belt but with enough of a drop so that the gun hangs at the bottom of the belt. Also, because of weight, I would appreciate it if you could drop four bullet loops on the right side and three on the left side of the buckle."

Wayne sent the belt and holster back, along with a simple drawing he scratched out for Bianchi, so he could see exactly how low he wanted the gun to hang below the belt. The exchange typified both Wayne's level of expertise and interest in firearms and his love of Western style. In fact, Western clothes (see page 46), Western and Native American art, horses, cattle, and ranching were interests that went far beyond his movie work.

Over the years, Wayne wore the stereotype of being a "cowboy star" as a badge of pride. He often spoke poetically of wanting to capture the pioneering spirit of the Old West in his movies, and he was always looking to make another Western. All told, he made eighty-four Western movies (see page 52). Some of his biggest professional achievements were Westerns: his first

PAGE 42: *John Wayne in* The Cowboys, *1972.* TOP: *Wayne enjoys a moment with his son, Patrick Wayne (left), on the set of* Hondo. LEFT: *The holster Wayne wore while starring in* El Dorado *in 1966.* OPPOSITE: *The letter John Wayne wrote to leather craftsman John Bianchi in 1978 about the design of a gun holster. Clipped to the letter is Wayne's simple sketch showing how he preferred the gun to "ride just below the belt."*

JOHN WAYNE

2686 Bayshore Drive
Newport Beach, California 92663
February 22, 1978

Mr. John E. Bianchi
100 Calle Cortez
Temecula, California 92390

Dear John:

I was most pleasantly surprised to open the package and
find the gun belt and holster. I immediately whipped it on
and found the belt fit perfectly.

You did ask for some suggestions. In order to make it handy
to get a gun out, I have always used a reinforced leather on the
front of my holster. Carry the holster over the gun belt but
with enough of a drop so that the gun hangs at the bottom of the
belt. Hope this drawing explains my words.

Also, because of weight, I would appreciate it if you could drop
four bullet loops on the right side and three on the left side of
the buckle.

I am enclosing your holster plus one shaped to my liking. If
you could make these corrections, I would be more than willing
to pay for the new setup.

Sincerely,

John Wayne

JW/ps

Enclosures

WESTERN GEAR

Since John Wayne appeared in more than eighty Westerns, it isn't surprising that he eventually developed a signature Western style and look, even as his wardrobe evolved over the decades. His surviving sons, both of whom worked on Westerns with him, say this signature look was painstakingly developed by Wayne both so he'd feel personally comfortable with how he looked on screen and to evoke a sense of realism.

"He always had the final say on what he wore," Patrick Wayne explains. "He was very sensitive about how he'd look on film. What kind of material the pants were made of was important—he was a big man and wanted a certain look. Certain things made him look bad, and he knew that—certain colors and different cuts. He liked to wear a vest over a shirt. For a cavalry outfit, he liked the suspenders in preference to the jacket—those double-breasted shirts. On jackets, he liked the collar up. He always wanted to wear a hat so light wouldn't cut through his eyes."

Ethan Wayne adds, "He also used some of the same clothing in multiple films, and it just became his look after a while. He was the most famous cowboy in the world, and yet he wasn't wearing fringe, and he didn't have nickel six-shooters. The stuff he wore was authentic and real. Everything he wore, he wore for a purpose. The pants and the belts were purposeful."

Indeed, some aspects of Wayne's wardrobe preferences became almost codified after a time. His necktie or kerchief, for instance, was usually knotted on the side, usually to the left, and he wore one particular red, white, and blue bandanna in several films after John Ford gave it to him while making *Stagecoach*. In several films, he wore the *Red River* logo belt buckle that first appeared in the 1948 film *Red River*. Off screen, he frequently wore a buckle of similar size and style—the 26 Bar Ranch buckle that was created in honor of the ranch he owned in Arizona with Louis Johnson (see page 49). After the early B-movie Western years, he started wearing a consistent hat style that was modeled loosely after a cavalry officer's hat design of the 1800s, including a dip in the brim, usually a leather band around the crown, and frequently light in color. His shirtsleeves were typically rolled up to the forearm, and shirts were always tucked in. All these decisions, and many others, were made in concert with costuming professionals, but always through his career, John Wayne had the final say on how he would look on screen.

Following are a sampling of images showing some of Wayne's best-known Western garb from different movies—all preserved and in safe-keeping at the John Wayne archives.

TOP: *A Western Costume Company clothing label with Wayne's measurements on it—Western Costume Company serviced dozens of his movies over the years.* PAGE 47: *The wardrobe continuity book from* Chisum, *1970. Such books are used to document with photos, measurements, and notes all kinds of wardrobe details for reference later, to ensure consistency in clothing seen on screen throughout a production.*

WESTERN
GEAR

★★★

OUTFITTING THE DUKE

[a.] *Shirt from* The Comancheros, *1961,* McLintock!, *1963, and* El Dorado, *1966.*
[b.] *Shirt from* True Grit, *1969.*
[c.] *Shirt from* True Grit, *1969.*
[d.] *Bib shirt from* The Man Who Shot Liberty Valance, *1962.*
[e.] *Bib shirt.*
[f.] *Shirt from* Big Jake, *1971.*
[g.] *Shirt from* Rooster Cogburn, *1975.*
[h.] *Shirt from* Rooster Cogburn, *1975.*

[a. & b.] *Vest from* True Grit, *1969.* [c. & d.] *Vest from* The Undefeated, *1969.* [e. & f.]*Vest from* Big Jake, *1971.*
[g.] *Vest from* Cahill, United States Marshal, *1973.*

a.

b.

c.

d.

e.

[a.] Stockade jacket from True Grit, 1969. *[b.] Stockade jacket from* North to Alaska, 1960, McLintock!, 1963, *and* The Sons of Katie Elder, 1965. *[c.] Stockade jacket from* Big Jake, 1971. *[d.] Stockade jacket from* Rooster Cogburn, 1975. *[e.] Jacket from* The War Wagon, 1967. *[f.] Jacket from* Chisum, 1970. *[g.] Coat from* North to Alaska, 1960. *[h.] Period jacket from* In Old California, 1942. *[i.] Period jacket from* Flame of Barbary Coast, 1945. *[j.] Period jacket and vest from* Flame of Barbary Coast, 1945. *[k.] Jacket and vest from* The Shootist, 1976.

[a.] *Pants from* The Comancheros, *1961.*
[b.] *Pants from* The Alamo, *1960.*
[c.] *Pants from* Rooster Cogburn, *1975.*
[d.] *Batwing chaps.*

[a.] *Costume from* The Cowboys, *1972.*
[b.] *Costume from* Rio Lobo, *1970.*
[c.] *Costume from* Chisum, *1970.*
[d.] *Costume from* Rio Lobo, *1970.*
[e.] *Costume from* Big Jake, *1971.*

[a.] *Costume from* The Train Robbers, *1973.*
[b.] *Costume from* The Cowboys, *1972.*
[c.] *Costume from* Rooster Cogburn, *1975.*
[d.] *Costume from* True Grit, *1969.*
[e.] *Costume from* Cahill, United States Marshal, *1973.*

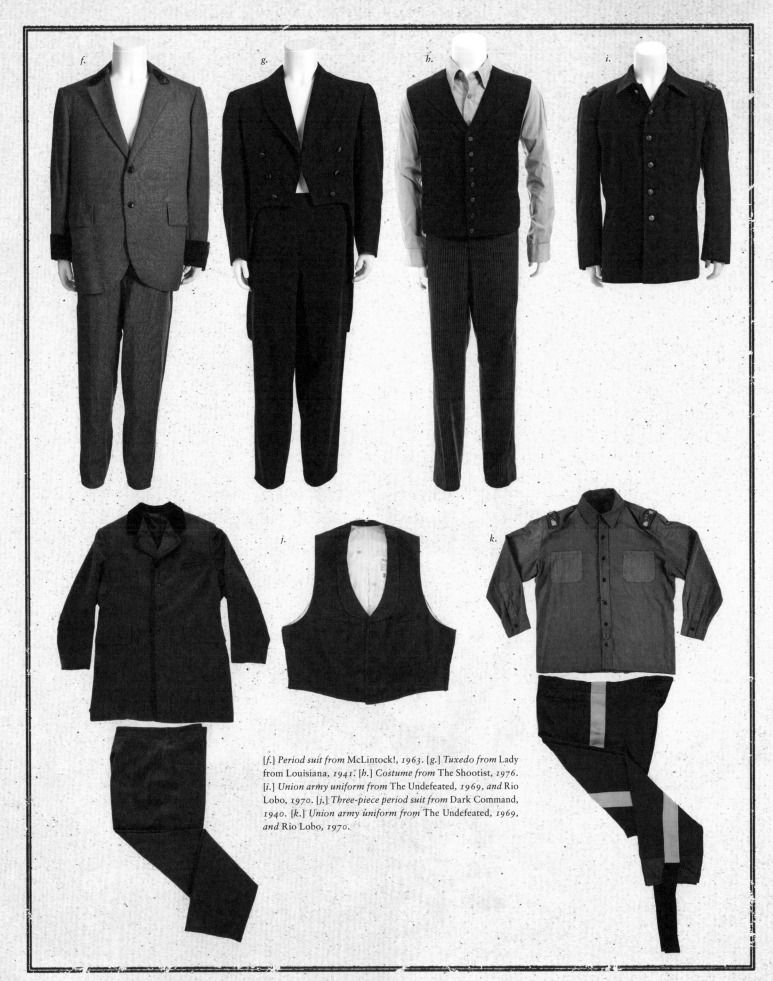

[f.] *Period suit from* McLintock!, *1963.* [g.] *Tuxedo from* Lady from Louisiana, *1941.* [h.] *Costume from* The Shootist, *1976.* [i.] *Union army uniform from* The Undefeated, *1969, and* Rio Lobo, *1970.* [j.] *Three-piece period suit from* Dark Command, *1940.* [k.] *Union army uniform from* The Undefeated, *1969, and* Rio Lobo, *1970.*

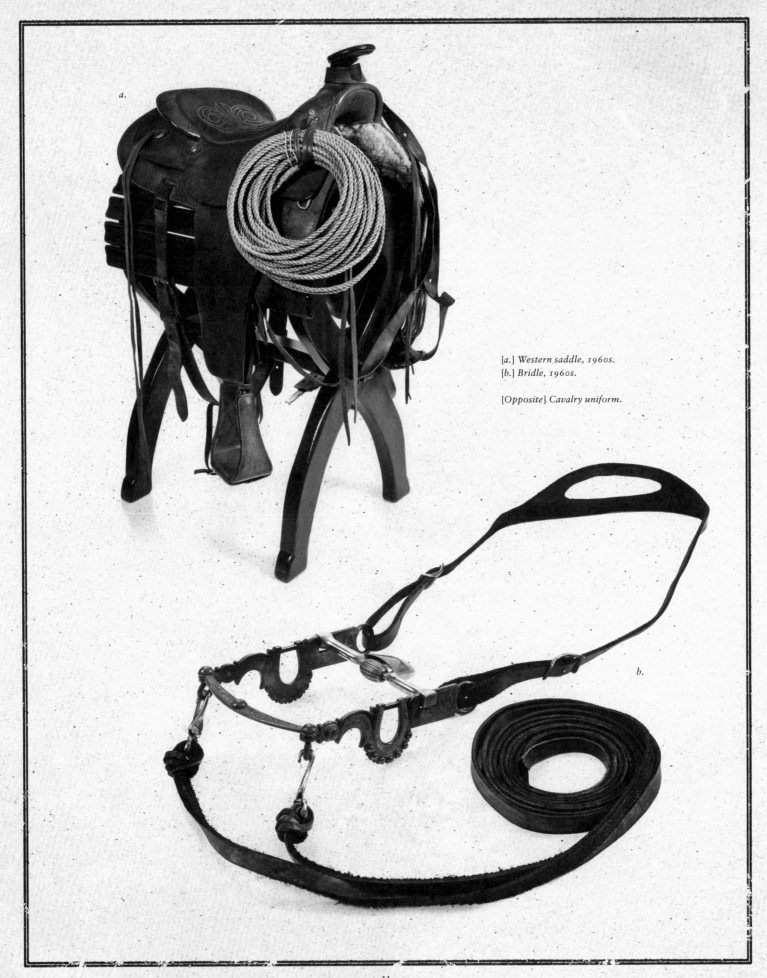

[a.] *Western saddle, 1960s.*
[b.] *Bridle, 1960s.*

[Opposite] *Cavalry uniform.*

[a.] *Stetson cowboy hat from* Hondo, *1953.* [b.] *Cowboy hat from* The Comancheros, *1961,* True Grit, *1969.* [c.] *Cavalry hat from* The Horse Soldiers, *1959,* Circus World, *1964,* The Undefeated, *1969,* Rio Lobo, *1970.* [d.] *Cowboy hat from* Big Jake, *1971,* The Cowboys, *1972, and* The Train Robbers, *1973.* [e.] *Nudie's cowboy hat from* Rooster Cogburn, *1975.* [f.] *Cowboy hat from* McLintock!, *1963,* El Dorado, *1966,* The War Wagon, *1967.* [g.] *Cowboy hat from* McLintock!, *1963,* El Dorado, *1966,* The War Wagon, *1967.* [h.] *Stetson cowboy hat from* The Man Who Shot Liberty Valance, *1962.* [i.] *Nudie's cowboy hat from* Cahill, United States Marshal, *1973.* [j.] *Two hatbands from* The Sons of Katie Elder, *1965.* [k.] *Nudie's cowboy hat, 1970s.* [l.] *Cowboy hat.*

f.

g.

h.

i.

j.

k.

l.

[a. & b.] Lucchese cowboy boots likely from True Grit, 1969, and Rooster Cogburn, 1975.
[c.] Nudie's cowboy boots, 1970s. [d.] Lucchese cowboy boots, 1970s. [e.] Nudie's cowboy boots, 1970s.
[f.] Lucchese cowboy boots, 1970s. [g.] Four boot jacks, 1960s–1970s. [h.] Cowboy boots.
[i.] Cowboy boots, 1960s–1970s. [j. & k.] Cavalry riding boots from The Undefeated, 1969.
[l.] Cowboy boots. [m.] Lucchese cowboy boots, 1970s. [n.] Boots, 1960s.

g.

h.

i.

j.

k.

l.

m.

n.

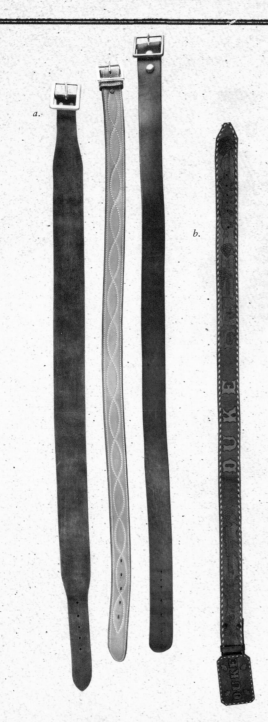

a.

b.

c.

d.

e.

f.

g.

h.

i.

[a.] Three Western belts, 1960s–1970s. [b.] "Duke" belt, 1970s.
[c.] Two "Duke" belts, 1970s. [d.] Three Western belts, 1950s–1970s.
[e.] "26 Bar Ranch" belt buckle, 1974. [f.] "The Cowboys" belt buckle, 1971.
[g.] "Red River D" belt buckle, 1946. Howard Hawks, the director of Red
River (1948), had silver belt buckles designed as gifts for some of the cast and
crew. John Wayne wore the buckle in a number of his later Westerns, including Rio Bravo, El Dorado, and Rio Lobo, all directed by Howard Hawks. The
two supposedly exchanged their respective, individualized belt buckles, as a
gesture of mutual respect and admiration. The buckle that Wayne wore had
the initials HWH encircled in the bottom left corner, and Hawks's buckle
had the initials JW.
[h.] "Go Texan" belt buckle, 1964. [i.] "26 Bar Ranch" buckle, 1976.
[j.] "Duke" belt, 1970s. [k.] "Duke" belt, 1978.

j.

k.

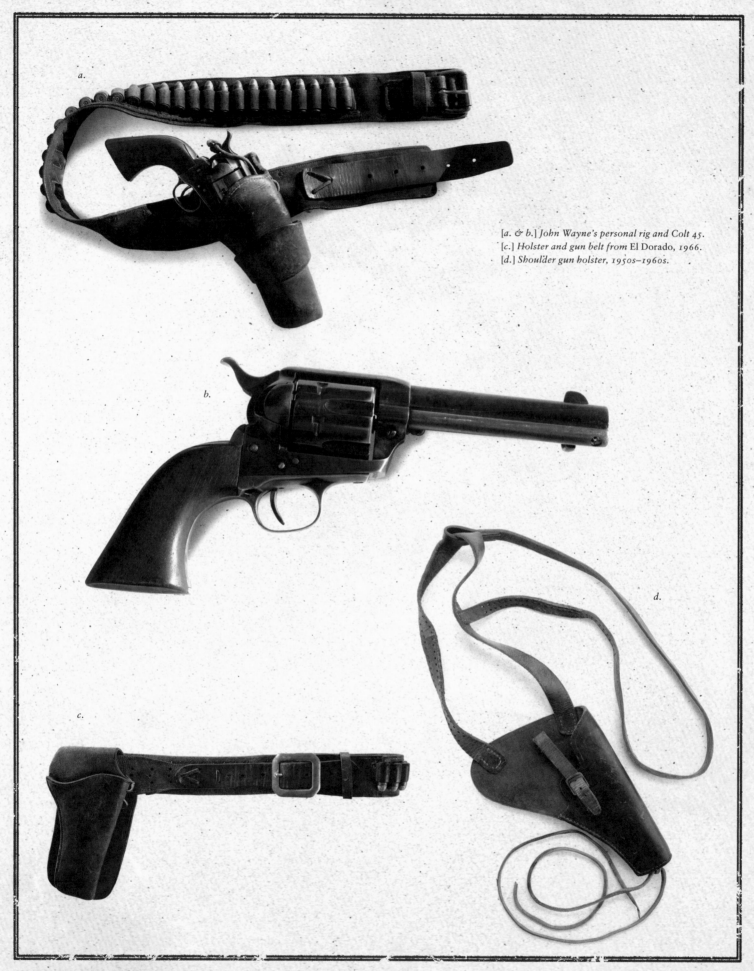

[a. & b.] John Wayne's personal rig and Colt 45.
[c.] Holster and gun belt from El Dorado, 1966.
[d.] Shoulder gun holster, 1950s–1960s.

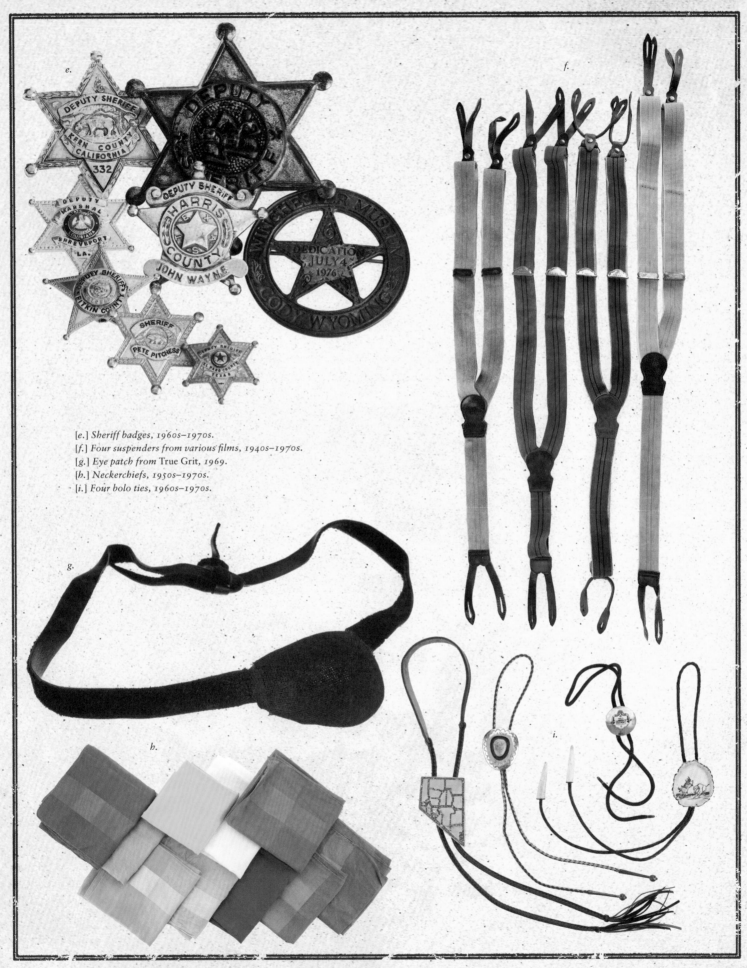

[e.] Sheriff badges, 1960s–1970s.
[f.] Four suspenders from various films, 1940s–1970s.
[g.] Eye patch from True Grit, 1969.
[h.] Neckerchiefs, 1950s–1970s.
[i.] Four bolo ties, 1960s–1970s.

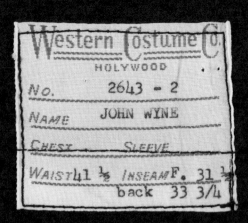

Western Costume Co.
HOLLYWOOD
NO. 2643 - 2
NAME JOHN WYNE
CHEST SLEEVE
WAIST 41½ INSEAM F. 31½
back 33 3/4

SyDevore
HOLLYWOOD
LAS VEGAS ★ PALM SPRINGS

Western Costume Co.
HOLLYWOOD
NO. 2227-1
NAME John Wayne
CHEST SLEEVE
WAIST INSEAM

Western Costume Co.
HOLLYWOOD
NO. 2660-5
NAME John Wayne #1
CHEST 45 SLEEVE
WAIST INSEAM

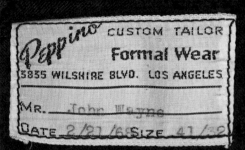

Peppino CUSTOM TAILOR
Formal Wear
3835 WILSHIRE BLVD. LOS ANGELES
MR. John Wayne
DATE 2/21/66 SIZE 41/32

AMERICAN COSTUME
NORTH HOLLYWOOD
MO#
NAME LUSTER BAYLESS
"PERSONAL"
SIZE

Western Costume Co.
HOLLYWOOD
NAME
CHEST SLEEVE
WAIST INSEAM

Western Costume Co.
HOLLYWOOD
NO. 2642 - 2
NAME JOHN WAYNE
CHEST 50 SLEEVE
WAIST INSEAM

Western Costume Co.
HOLLYWOOD
NO.
NAME
CHEST SLEEVE
WAIST INSEAM

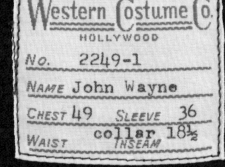

Western Costume Co.
HOLLYWOOD
NO. 2249-1
NAME John Wayne
CHEST 49 SLEEVE 36
collar 18½
WAIST INSEAM

Western Costume Co.
HOLLYWOOD
NO.
NAME John Wayne
CHEST 49 SLEEVE 36
collar 18½
WAIST INSEAM

Western Costume Co.
HOLLYWOOD
NO. 2354-4
NAME John Wayne #1
CHEST 46 SLEEVE
WAIST INSEAM

John Galuppo
BEVERLY HILLS

Western Costume Co.
HOLLYWOOD
NO. 2869-2
NAME John Wayne #1
CHEST SLEEVE
WAIST 40½ INSEAM

Western Costume Co.
HOLLYWOOD
NO. 2655 - 1
NAME JOHN WAYNE
CHEST SLEEVE 34
collar 18½
WAIST INSEAM

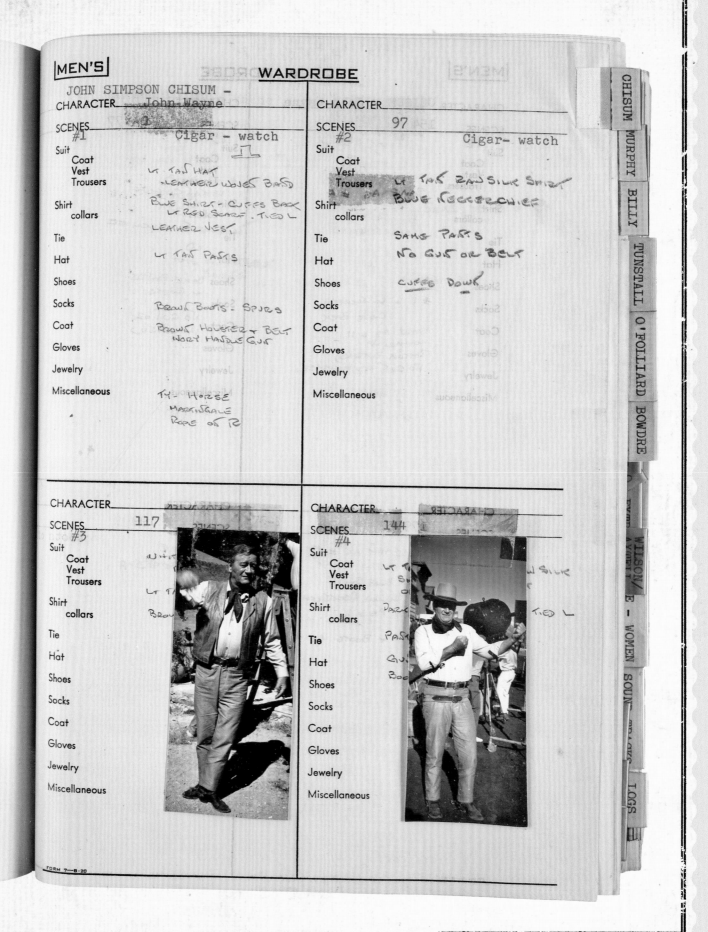

CHARACTER JOHN SIMPSON CHISUM – John Wayne

SCENES #1   Cigar – watch

Suit	
Coat	
Vest	Lt Tan Hat
Trousers	Leather woven band
Shirt	Blue Shirt - Cuffs Back
collars	Lt Red Scarf. Tied L
Tie	Leather Vest
Hat	Lt Tan Pants
Shoes	
Socks	Brown Boots - Spurs
Coat	Brown Holster + Belt
Gloves	Ivory Handle Gun
Jewelry	
Miscellaneous	Ty - Horse
	Martingale
	Rope of R

CHARACTER

SCENES 97   Cigar- watch

Suit	
Coat	
Vest	Lt Tan Tan Silk Shirt
Trousers	
Shirt	Blue Neckerchief
collars	
Tie	Same Pants
Hat	No Gun or Belt
Shoes	Cuffs Down
Socks	
Coat	
Gloves	
Jewelry	
Miscellaneous	

CHARACTER

SCENES 117   #3

Suit	
Coat	
Vest	
Trousers	Lt Ta
Shirt	
collars	Bro
Tie	
Hat	
Shoes	
Socks	
Coat	
Gloves	
Jewelry	
Miscellaneous	

CHARACTER

SCENES 144   #4

Suit	
Coat	Lt T
Vest	S
Trousers	
Shirt	Dark
collars	
Tie	Pas
Hat	Gu
Shoes	Bo
Socks	
Coat	
Gloves	
Jewelry	
Miscellaneous	

FORM 7—8—20

Tabs: CHISUM   MURPHY   BILLY   TUNSTALL   O'FOLLIARD   BOWDRE   WILSON/E   AYTETTE   WOMEN   SOUND   LOGS

hit, *Stagecoach*, immediately became a classic in the genre; he won the Best Actor Academy Award for *True Grit*; and perhaps his most moving performance ever was in his final film, *The Shootist*.

For those movies, Wayne worked hard to make his costumes realistic and his riding and shooting skillful. How he wore his gun belt, hat, kerchief, how he rode a horse—all these things were based on observations of real cowboys or actors or stuntmen he knew, whose mannerisms or style he chose to emulate. He became almost obsessive about this aspect of his craft, and he became so associated with certain looks, in fact, that boot and hat manufacturers, like Stetson, periodically hired him to endorse their products.

John Wayne's love of Western themes was not about simply promulgating an image. He *really* loved the West. His heartfelt belief was that America's frontier was, back in the day, a place of wide-open spaces where pioneering acts of heroism and adventure occurred in pursuit of a better life. He found such notions enchanting, romantic, and inspiring. In fact, in 1973, he made these feelings quite clear during the making of the Grammy-nominated, patriotic spoken-word album called *America: Why I Love Her*, for which he recited poetry written by John Mitchum.

One of the album's subjects was the lure of the West, and in a poem called "*Mis Raices Estan Aqui* (My Roots Are Buried Here)," he read Mitchum's eloquent words—an ode to pioneers

who tamed the land and put down roots despite enormous challenges. A few years later, in 1977, a tie-in book was published, featuring essays penned by Wayne on topics from the original album, along with Mitchum's poetry and music written by Billy Leibert from the album. In the John Wayne archives, a draft version of Wayne's essays includes his thoughts from the "*Mis Raices Estan Aqui*" chapter. That essay starts with Wayne plainly stating, "For me, to deny a lifelong love of the West would be impossible."

The essay continues: "In the last forty years I've ridden over a lot of territory on horseback and from up close you can see just how tough the Southwest deserts can be. The ancient Arizona mountains have been worn down by blowing winds for tens of

Form F.   C.A.R.

N° 30170

FIRE-ARM LICENCE

The Arms and Ammunition Ordinance (Cap. 223)
The Arms and Ammunition Regulations (Regulations 12(2))

THIS LICENCE MUST BE RENEWED ANNUALLY ON 1ST APRIL

ANY PERSON FINDING THIS FIRE-ARM LICENCE IS REQUESTED TO HAND IT OR SEND IT TO THE NEAREST POLICE STATION

f New Mexico's
against the clear
he blood of the
harsh, yet beau-

had poetic impli-
phy manuscript,
action is a horse.
out photographi-
se. Horses mean

ckles that riding
that his father

xample, but his
on *Comanche-*
a close-up, with
ins. "The dailies
My dad, in front
se or get out of
this business.' I was embarrassed, but I started riding every free moment, and I did learn. It was the kind of broad lesson he liked to teach—if you have to do something physical on a film, you better be prepared and have it down ice cold. For him, it was more natural—I had to work on it, but that taught me a great lesson."

As his career went on, John Wayne also grew increasingly concerned with the welfare of the horses that appeared in his films. In 1973, he agreed to serve as national kindness chairman for the American Humane Association's Be Kind to Animals Week. In one famous picture, he posed in cowboy garb with a poster for the Be Kind to Animals event, which was circulated to the media, and he also was featured on the cover of the February 1973 issue of *Animal Shelter Shoptalk*, a trade publication for the animal-care community.

In the campaign, he declared, "When I first began making Westerns, they said the cowboy only shook hands with the girl and kissed the horse. I never really kissed any of my horses, but I will say I appreciated every one of them and I've always seen to it that they get the best of care."

In fact, livestock were among Wayne's big interests, starting with probably his most successful, non-movie-related business venture—his beloved 26 Bar Ranch in Casa Grande, Arizona. Wayne and his partner, Louis Johnson, owned more than fourteen thousand acres (in the Casa Grande area, where the feed lot

and ranch headquarters were), and also grazed cattle each summer on leased government land in the area around Springerville, Arizona. Their operation also included growing twelve thousand acres of cotton in nearby Stanfield, Arizona. Each year at the ranch, John Wayne would preside over an annual Thanksgiving bull auction, cracking jokes and doing what he could to help Johnson drive up the price of their prize Hereford bulls.

"Bulls go to the highest bidders, which makes it a lot like politics," he chuckled during the 1973 auction. "The only trouble is that in politics they have a lot more bull to sell than we'll ever have."

In truth, the 26 Bar Ranch was a successful working ranch operated by Johnson, who remained Wayne's close associate until the end of his life and served as one of the executors of his will. Wayne was steadfastly appreciative of Louis Johnson's stewardship. "Louis Johnson is my partner in Arizona," he told journalist Wayne Warga in 1969. "He gives better than he gets—that's the

---

OPPOSITE, TOP: *John Wayne rides through desert sand in* The Train Robbers. OPPOSITE, BOTTOM: *Leading his horse through Monument Valley, on location for* Rio Grande. BELOW: *John Wayne poses with a favorite shotgun he used for hunting, one of more than sixty guns from his collection.*

"The Duke". Colt's tribute to the hero in everyone.

In the minds of a nation, John Wayne is remembered in many ways. To some, he's Hondo, McLintock and the legendary Rooster Cogburn. To others, he's simply "Duke". But to everyone, he represents a hero. One of the greatest of them all.

On-screen, John Wayne's ability to handle a gun helped tame the West. Off-screen, he was a skilled marksman who used and collected handguns and rifles. In keeping with this American tradition, Colt and the Wayne family are proud to introduce "The Duke". A limited edition, .22 caliber single action frontier revolver.

Rugged and handsome, this special edition can be acquired as a collector's item. But, like every Colt, it's a working gun. Use it. Take it to the range. It features a 4-2/5" blued barrel, handsomely etched with sterling silver plated inscription "John Wayne, The Duke". Each gun features the famous Colt color case-hardened frame, an adjustable rear sight, and a unique blade front sight, in keeping with the original "frontier peacemaker". Its deep blue finish is accentuated by a nickel ejector rod, trigger and hammer.

And each special edition gun is also accompanied by a custom presentation case, with a sterling silver plated plaque distinctively etched with a portrait of John Wayne and the house in Winterset, Iowa where he was born.

The price of this special edition is less than you'd expect. $475 suggested retail price. Ask your gun dealer about "The Duke". Enjoy it, use it, and be proud of it. With all the hero that's in you.

A portion of the proceeds from the sale of each special edition of "The Duke" will be donated to the John Wayne Cancer Clinic, UCLA Medical Center, Los Angeles, California.

COLT An Investment in Precision
Hartford, CT 06101

Be a safe shooter—never chamber a round until you are ready to shoot. Always read and follow the instruction manuals which accompany each firearm. Free instruction manuals are available from the factory on request.

kind of man he is." At that same 1973 bull auction at the ranch, Wayne closed his remarks by publicly paying tribute to Johnson.

"And I guess I am most of all thankful to my partner, Louie Johnson, who is truly the anchor man in my life," he declared.

Wayne was also actively involved in the venture. At one point, according to his daughter Melinda Wayne Munoz, he paid close attention when a young livestock equipment designer by the name of Temple Grandin visited the ranch with some suggestions. Grandin had a design for livestock feeding and handling technologies that she felt would be more humane for livestock being raised for slaughter. The design involved changing the long-held approach to cattle handling facilities by curving grazing lanes to honor the cattle's inherent instinct to walk in a circular pattern. Grandin devised a curved lane leading into a dip vat for the cattle at the 26 Bar Ranch feed yard that eventually was adapted for not only ranches, but meat packing plants, as well.

"She told [ranch management] that the cattle were scared and stressed, and told them she could fix that," Melinda remembers.

TOP LEFT: *John Wayne featured in a print advertisement for Colt handguns. Wayne also endorsed Western hats and boots, among other items.* OPPOSITE, TOP: *John Wayne featured on the* Life *magazine cover in 1965, an honor he was given while recovering from his 1964 cancer surgery.* OPPOSITE, BOTTOM: *Cowboy Hall of Fame Wrangler Award, presented in 1961 to honor* The Alamo.

"So she invented this chute so the cattle could follow each other. My father was visiting and asked her to put it in at his ranch."

Grandin went on to become famous in her own right. Among her many achievements, she is today a world-renowned lecturer on the subjects of animal husbandry, animal rights, and high-functioning autism; she is a best-selling author, a professor of animal science at Colorado State University, and was the subject of a 2010 feature film. But she was just launching her career when Wayne and Louis Johnson progressively welcomed her ideas at the 26 Bar Ranch. Those designs were part of her earliest professional work—work that was later widely adopted in the livestock industry and a major breakthrough in a field hardly open to women before Grandin came along.

As important as the business of ranching, lots of fun was had on the ranch, and Wayne encouraged his children to embrace a Western lifestyle. Today, Wayne family members all have fond memories of visiting the ranch in their younger days.

"We all loved going to the ranch because it was another kind of setting, another kind of people," his wife, Pilar, explains. "The kids could ride horses and go hunting—different from what they could do in Newport Beach, obviously. And every Thanksgiving, we all went for the cattle sale—it was an auction and a huge Thanksgiving dinner."

Son Ethan Wayne adds, "We did enjoy the 26 Bar Ranch, but for riding horses and learning about ranch work, we also went to another ranch—Ralph Wingfield's place in Nogales." Now called the Hacienda Corona de Guevavi, Wingfield's land in New Mexico was where Wayne's *Red River* was shot in 1948, and from that point on, the Waynes would periodically return there on Wingfield's invitation for rest and relaxation.

Perhaps because he was involved in the ranching business, Wayne also developed an abiding interest in issues of importance to ranchers, particularly the well-being of the American beef industry. For instance, in 1972, right after the reelection of Richard Nixon, Wayne wrote Nixon a letter to express concern about the issue of unrestrained cattle imports. He enclosed his recent correspondence with officials at the American National Cattlemen's Association about their fears over unlimited imports of foreign cattle, and he asked Nixon to "assign" the letter to "some responsible member of your administration" to review.

Indeed, Secretary of Agriculture Earl Butz reviewed the situation and wrote Wayne back in February 1973; he explained in detail why the lack of restraints on cattle prices was appropriate at that time in terms of protecting consumers. Wayne remained concerned about the issue, and in January 1975, he wrote a two-page letter to President Gerald Ford to express his views. In that letter, he suggested, "Cattlemen are going broke with an oversupply of beef. We also have people out of work and a food stamp program." He proposed addressing both problems by having the government step in and buy the oversupply of beef, can it, and distribute it to those on food stamps.

"[Such an idea] would also provide much employment and give an industry a chance to re-adjust itself," he added. "We have about 6 percent of our population in agriculture, and we better keep them in it."

Another beloved aspect of Western life that eventually led Wayne to take a political stance (as we'll see in Chapter Six) was firearms. However, politics aside and on a personal level, Wayne was expert in their use, had a large collection, and periodically hunted over the years. At one point, late in his life, Wayne's collection numbered well over sixty guns, which were locked in glass cases in his den in Newport Beach. A large percentage of them were stolen from his house during a break-in in 1971, and soon after some were recovered in a police raid in Mexico. The *Orange County Register* newspaper ran an article in March 1971 showing a smiling Wayne at the police station, holding one of his repatriated weapons. He got back his prized Weatherby .22-caliber long rifle and Weatherby .300 Magnum rifle, both of which had "Duke" inscribed on the handle. But his favored Pachmayr .270 special rifle, which had been custom-made for him almost forty years earlier, never turned up.

The den in Wayne's Newport Beach home was also lined with his collection of Native American kachina dolls. He first became

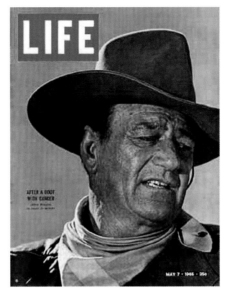

interested in the collectible dolls around the time he made *Stagecoach* in Monument Valley, a location he would return to over the years that is within the Navajo Indian reservation. Authentic Hopi kachinas are religious icons; they are colorful figurines decorated in the likeness of spirits and supernatural deities (though they are made by several tribes). Over time, Wayne collected more than sixty kachina dolls, displaying them proudly on a ledge high along one wall in his den, and he would regale people with stories about when and how he got particular dolls, what they meant to the Hopi, why they were interesting to him, and so on.

Kachina dolls were not the only Native American artifacts Wayne collected, and he often showed interest in Native American culture. In 1971, when he returned to Monument Valley to film a CBS television special called *The American West of John Ford* to honor his old friend, he particularly appreciated meeting up again with local natives who had worked with his *Stagecoach* crew many years before. According to Wayne Warga's notes for Wayne's biography manuscript, in fact, Wayne enjoyed a barbecue in his and Ford's honor thrown by local Navajos on the reservation where the TV special was being filmed.

Warga was present during the barbecue, and in his first-person account, he wrote that "both Wayne and Ford give brief speeches in the Navajo language. Then Wayne obligingly poses for pictures with all the children and with several of their grandparents whom he and Ford have known for many years and many pictures." ✪

HALL OF FAMER

Upon John Wayne's death, his kachina doll collection, along with other artwork, guns, knives, and movie memorabilia, were donated to the National Cowboy & Western Heritage Museum in Oklahoma City, where he had served for years on the board of trustees. The museum inducted Wayne into the performer's division of its Hall of Fame in 1974, and his portrait and statue are on display there, along with his collections. The donation also included Wyoming artist Harry Jackson's painted bronze of Wayne from his famous role as Rooster Cogburn in *True Grit* and the iron ring Winchester rifle he used in multiple films, including *Stagecoach* and *Red River*.

JOHN WAYNE'S WESTERNS

Few actors, if any, are more closely associated with a particular genre than John Wayne is with the Western. Starting in 1930, when he got a lead role in *The Big Trail*, to 1976, when he gave his final performance in *The Shootist,* he performed in eighty-four Westerns in which he had significant speaking roles. Prior to 1940, many of them were of the so-called "quickie Western" variety—one-reel shorts, sometimes in a serial format, with several being made in a single year. But even from *Stagecoach* (1939) onward, when he graduated from the B-movie category to major features, he made a stunning thirty-nine full-length Western features over the course of his remarkable career.

Following is a list of all of John Wayne's Western movies:

The Big Trail (1930)	*Winds of the Wasteland* (1936)	*The Fighting Kentuckian* (1949)
The Range Feud (1931)	*The Lonely Trail* (1936)	*She Wore a Yellow Ribbon* (1949)
Two-Fisted Law (1932)	*The Lawless Nineties* (1936)	*Rio Grande* (1950)
Texas Cyclone (1932)	*King of the Pecos* (1936)	*Hondo* (1953)
Ride Him, Cowboy (1932)	*California Straight Ahead!* (1937)	*The Searchers* (1956)
Haunted Gold (1932)	*Born to the West* (1937)	*The Horse Soldiers* (1959)
The Big Stampede (1932)	*Santa Fe Stampede* (1938)	*Rio Bravo* (1959)
The Telegraph Trail (1933)	*Red River Range* (1938)	*The Alamo* (1960)
Somewhere in Sonora (1933)	*Pals of the Saddle* (1938)	*North to Alaska* (1960)
Sagebrush Trail (1933)	*Overland Stage Raiders* (1938)	*The Comancheros* (1961)
Riders of Destiny (1933)	*Wyoming Outlaw* (1939)	*How the West Was Won* (1962)
The Man from Monterey (1933)	*Three Texas Steers* (1939)	*The Man Who Shot Liberty*
West of the Divide (1934)	*The Night Riders* (1939)	*Valance* (1962)
The Trail Beyond (1934)	*New Frontier* (1939)	*McLintock!* (1963)
The Star Packer (1934)	*Allegheny Uprising* (1939)	*The Sons of Katie Elder* (1965)
Randy Rides Alone (1934)	*Stagecoach* (1939)	*El Dorado* (1966)
The Man from Utah (1934)	*Dark Command* (1940)	*The War Wagon* (1967)
The Lucky Texan (1934)	*Lady from Louisiana* (1941)	*True Grit* (1969)
The Lawless Frontier (1934)	*The Spoilers* (1942)	*The Undefeated* (1969)
Blue Steel (1934)	*In Old California* (1942)	*Chisum* (1970)
'Neath the Arizona Skies (1934)	*A Lady Takes a Chance* (1943)	*Rio Lobo* (1970)
Westward Ho (1935)	*In Old Oklahoma* (1943)	*Big Jake* (1971)
Texas Terror (1935)	*Tall in the Saddle* (1944)	*The Cowboys* (1972)
Rainbow Valley (1935)	*Dakota* (1945)	*Cahill, United States Marshal* (1973)
Paradise Canyon (1935)	*Flame of Barbary Coast* (1945)	*The Train Robbers* (1973)
The New Frontier (1935)	*Angel and the Badman* (1947)	*Rooster Cogburn* (1975)
Lawless Range (1935)	*3 Godfathers* (1948)	*The Shootist* (1976)
The Desert Trail (1935)	*Fort Apache* (1948)	
The Dawn Rider (1935)	*Red River* (1948)	

OPPOSITE: *Items indicative of John Wayne's western film work, including movie posters from* War of the Wildcats, El Dorado, *and* Sagebrush Trail, *and script covers of* The Searchers *and* She Wore a Yellow Ribbon. TOP RIGHT: *A scene from* Stagecoach, *with Claire Trevor.* LEFT: *Wayne in* The Comancheros. BOTTOM CENTER: *Wayne with his son Patrick from* The Searchers. BOTTOM RIGHT: *Wayne as Rooster Cogburn from* True Grit.

JOHN WAYNE ★ MARTHA SCOTT

WAR OF THE WILDCATS

(Formerly Entitled "In Old Oklahoma")
by Thomson Burtis

with ALBERT DEKKER

A REPUBLIC PICTURE

THE SEARCHERS

JW

IT'S THE BIG ONE WITH THE BIG TWO

HOWARD HAWKS
presents

JOHN WAYNE
IS THE GUNFIGHTER

ROBERT MITCHUM
IS THE SHERIFF

They were friends. They were enemies. A passerby could not tell which was who. This was the seething sultry Old Southwest. Where loyalties and labels shifted with the sands, the winking of an eye, the wavering of a gun!

EL DORADO

JAMES CAAN · CHARLENE HOLT · PAUL FIX · ARTHUR HUNNICUTT · MICHELE CAREY

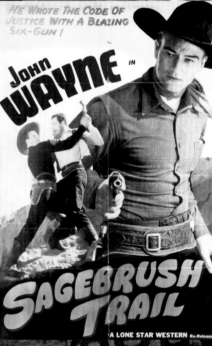

HE WROTE THE CODE OF JUSTICE WITH A BLAZING SIX-GUN!

JOHN WAYNE IN

SAGEBRUSH TRAIL

A LONE STAR WESTERN Re-Release

"SHE WORE A YELLOW RIBBON"
Shooting Script
October 16, 1948

SHOOTING SCRIPT

CHAPTER FOUR

OUR GLORIOUS INDUSTRY

"I'VE BEEN IN MORE UNIFORMS THAN GEORGIE JESSEL.
I'VE BEEN IN MORE BATTLES THAN NAPOLÉON, AND MORE
WARS THAN GERMANY. I'VE CAPTURED BATAAN, CORREGIDOR,
FORT APACHE, AND MAUREEN O'HARA."
—JOHN WAYNE, NFL FOUNDATION SPEECH, DECEMBER 10, 1974

I N 1970, SHORTLY AFTER WINNING AN ACADEMY AWARD for his performance as the eyepatch-wearing Rooster Cogburn in *True Grit*, John Wayne returned to Arizona to finish shooting *Rio Lobo*, where he was greeted by what he said was "the damnedest thing I ever saw." What he saw, according to an article by Peter J. Oppenheimer, was about two hundred cast and crew members of *Rio Lobo* waiting for him in front of an old church in Tucson, where the movie was being shot—all wearing Rooster Cogburn–style eyepatches in his honor, at the behest of *Rio Lobo* director Howard Hawks, his friend.

"Even the horses were wearing eyepatches!" Wayne told Oppenheimer. He was clearly moved and admitted that he "sure as hell wanted to win" what had, until that year, been an elusive honor that had escaped his grasp. In accepting his Oscar from Barbra Streisand, Wayne humbly thanked the Academy, a few specific people, and then the millions watching at home on television for "taking such a warm interest in our glorious industry."

Congratulatory telegrams poured in to the Wayne household to mark his achievement, and for days afterward, from a hotel room in Arizona, John Wayne

spent hours politely writing thank-you cards to people as diverse as his Hollywood chums, former president Lyndon Johnson, and Prince Rainier and Princess Grace of Monaco, among others.

It was a highly emotional time for him. The recognition Wayne had always sought from his peers was tempered by a deep loss a few weeks earlier, when his

PAGE 54: *John Wayne in a personalized set chair— the motion picture business was, without a doubt, his passion.* TOP: *John Wayne with costars on the set of* True Grit. LEFT: *John Wayne shares a tender moment with his mother, Mary, whom he often called Molly Brown.* OPPOSITE: *John Wayne celebrates his* True Grit *Oscar with presenter Barbra Streisand in 1970 at the Dorothy Chandler Pavilion.*

OUR GLORIOUS INDUSTRY

mother passed away—"my Molly Brown," he is quoted as telling Oppenheimer. Then, Wayne's brother, Robert, died a couple of months later. Yet Wayne kept as busy as ever preparing two more Westerns for release in 1970, *Chisum* and *Rio Lobo*.

He was at the height of his fame and thoroughly absorbed with his "beloved industry." In fact, although he tried his hand at a variety of businesses—ranging from mining to shrimp boats to oil wells and ranching—with varying degrees of success, Wayne was only truly *passionate* about the motion-picture business, insists his son Patrick.

"In other businesses, he would find a [partner] and trust that person to do what they said they would do, and he didn't always pay that much attention to it after that," Patrick explains. "But that's because his focus was always on filmmaking, on developing his craft, and working on films. That is where he was most comfortable. My father was more than a movie star—he was a filmmaker, a producer, and a director, and he was involved in all aspects of filmmaking, even when he didn't get credit for it. That is where his passion was."

Wayne's archives contain dozens of his original scripts from various films over the years, many marked up with notes from him in pencil. He was always searching for projects,

hiring writers, and producing films through his two production companies—Wayne-Fellows and later Batjac. He usually involved himself in every aspect of a film's development, and he labored hard to make his voice heard on how each film was distributed, marketed, and even exhibited.

"After 38 years in this business, I should be able to recognize a box office winner," he wrote Tom Moyer of the Moyer Theaters exhibition chain on February 27, 1967, to drum up enthusiasm for his latest picture. "*The War Wagon* will pack them in for you."

Before that picture was released, Wayne even appeared in a 1966 episode of *The Lucy Show* in an episode titled "Lucy and John Wayne," good-naturedly participating in a silly sitcom plot entangling him with Lucille Ball's character during filming of *The War Wagon*.

TOP: *Four of the main awards John Wayne displayed in his home. Left to right: His Cecil B. DeMille Award for Lifetime Achievement from the Hollywood Foreign Press Association in 1966; his Golden Globe Award for* True Grit; *his 1970 Academy Award for that same performance; and his 1976 People's Choice Award.* RIGHT: *A coonskin-capped John Wayne promotes Popsicles as part of the innovative marketing campaign for* The Alamo *in 1960.* OPPOSITE: *With Lucille Ball and Vivian Vance. John Wayne appeared on* I Love Lucy *in 1955 and* The Lucy Show *in 1966.*

59

60

Promoting his pictures was old hat for John Wayne. In 1960, he did a series of advertisements and comic books to push *The Alamo,* including print ads of Wayne, in character, promoting Popsicles. Advertising maven Russell Birdwell masterminded those ads, and he sent over a picture that still resides in the Wayne archives today, reminding Wayne that a much younger version of himself from his B-movie days had posed for similar advertisements for Sherbicles, a now-defunct type of Popsicle. Wayne had Birdwell produce an elaborate press kit and promote the notion of "Alamo Day" in several states and in elementary schools across the nation.

A few years earlier, to promote *The Searchers,* Wayne went on an East Coast junket to talk to the press, which included sit-downs with radio and television people in Chicago, Detroit, Cleveland, and Buffalo, among other places. Afterward, on May 25, 1956, Warner Brothers' public relations man Frank Casey sent Wayne a list summarizing every press person he had met, with notations about their interactions and suggestions for thank-you notes and gifts. The studio clearly felt that personal dealings with John Wayne would help generate positive buzz for the film.

Regarding Chicago radio personality Howard Miller, Casey suggested to Wayne that "it would be worth sending Howard some type of an inexpensive gift, …maybe a couple of ties from Saks Fifth Avenue or if you could find some kind of a gimmick (such as an ashtray, etc.), which would be suitable for a boat, as Howard has a 50-foot Chris-Craft cabin cruiser. The thought, and coming from you, is more important than the value."

Those kind of personal touches were common with the Hollywood press back then, and Wayne was expert at that game. Indeed, his archives feature numerous letters between Wayne and such Hollywood press luminaries as Walter Winchell, Louella Parsons, Hedda Hopper, Army Archerd, publisher Otis Chandler of the *Los Angeles Times,* and many others. Wayne would regularly write Winchell in the late 1950s and early 1960s to thank him for positive mentions in his columns and to periodically pat him on the back for his conservative political stances.

"Dear Walter," he wrote Winchell in 1953. "Thanks for the nice things about *Hondo.* I don't want to seem melodramatic but my deepest thanks for what you say for the good of our country."

Wayne didn't just support his movies—he helped plan and improve them when possible. And he wasn't shy about offering advice, whether asked or not. On January 28, 1969, in fact, he critiqued the evolving version of *True Grit* in one of many letters he wrote to the film's producer, Hal Wallis. He loved where the film was going, and he sensed they had a winner on their hands, but he still had two pages of proposed tweaks.

"I feel that the little girl does not hit her stride until she gets to the town at the hanging," he wrote regarding a key early moment in the film. "And since on three different occasions she explains what happened to her father, I had the feeling you could, with some re-cutting, avoid the use of the first episode. Or, if the gambling scene has some more cuts, that would build up suspense and an intelligent understanding of what was going on in the game, perhaps the picture could start there. The way it is cut now, the gambling inside and shooting outside are neither fish nor fowl, in my humble opinion."

Five years later, on May 21, 1974, Wayne wrote Wallis again, this time about *True Grit*'s upcoming sequel, *Rooster Cogburn.* His note suggested trepidation at the casting of the immortal Katharine Hepburn as his costar. Wayne told Wallis, "I can't think of anything that would give me more of a thrill than working with Miss Hepburn. God knows that for sophisticated theater goers, this would be a far-out combination." However, he continued, "To the people under 30 years old the combination won't mean anything but two older people in a picture. Using someone like Mary Tyler Moore or another actress in her age group, with whom the audience can identify, would appeal more to the age group we are trying to sell."

Hepburn was ultimately chosen for the part, of course, and to great acclaim. But that was hardly the only casting suggestion Wayne ever made. Singer Glen Campbell, for instance, was essentially handpicked by Wayne to play the role of La Boeuf in *True Grit.* In interviews over the years, Campbell said this was largely because one of Wayne's daughters was fond of his music.

"I told him I'd never acted before, and he said, 'I'll drag you through it—it'll be all right,'" Campbell told an interviewer during a tribute to Wayne in November 2011.

In 1966, before Kirk Douglas won the role of Lomax in *The War Wagon,* Wayne sent a letter to acting legend Richard Burton in Rome, suggesting Burton consider taking the role opposite Wayne in the Western revenge picture.

"I feel you could kick the hell out of the Lomax role, and the characters Lomax and Jackson [Wayne's character] lend themselves to humor and a wild, untamed relationship," he wrote Burton. "This is the first two-man story I have ever read in which

---

OPPOSITE: *John Wayne as Rooster Cogburn and Katharine Hepburn as Eula Goodnight in* Rooster Cogburn. *Wayne at first thought their pairing wouldn't attract younger audiences, but the two legends thoroughly enjoyed working together.*

both men have equal parts. I find each part is colorful without being similar. Add to this the action, production, and scenic values inherent in a good Western, and I think it will be an exciting picture—and with our two names on the marquee, who knows what the hell it could do!"

As he did with *True Grit*, and dozens of films before that over the years, Wayne typically inserted himself deeply in the details of developing, shooting, and producing his films, suggesting tweaks and improvements routinely, and expecting people to, at a minimum, listen to what he had to say. This was certainly true with the aforementioned *Rooster Cogburn*. On that project, despite how much he enjoyed working with Katharine Hepburn, Wayne was not particularly pleased with how the movie was developing as production wore on. One night, on October 8, 1974, unable to sleep, he took the rare step of sitting down at a typewriter himself to knock out another letter to Wallis, expressing his frustrations with director Stuart Millar. The three-page missive, filled with typos, told of his disappointment that the

movie was not hitting the quality level of *True Grit* and that Millar was not giving Wayne's experience and suggestions proper consideration. Still, Wayne made a point of emphasizing to Wallis that he fully understood and supported the project's need to emphasize Hepburn's character, Eula Goodnight, over his own.

"Quite obviously when you [have] a strong character like Miss Hepburn and you want to make her happy and get a good part for her [it is] necessary to adjust scenes," he wrote Wallis. "This was done and in many places at the beginnings and ends

TOP: *John Wayne visits Colorado with friend and periodic colleague, director Henry Hathaway.* RIGHT: *With Yvonne De Carlo in* McLintock! OPPOSITE: *John Wayne's personal scripts, with his own notes on the pages, from* Hellfighters *(top) and* The Shootist *(bottom).*

of scenes, the Cogburn character was neglected. This is quite natural. I was not upset about it one bit. I just presumed that we would have a chance to discuss these things when they came up."

During development of *McLintock!,* Wayne wrote an interesting letter on August 28, 1962, to Henry Hathaway, an old friend and collaborator, asking for the director's input on the film's script even though Hathaway had no connection to the film. Wayne proceeded to describe for Hathaway his desire to add a "drunk" scene between his character, McLintock, and Yvonne De Carlo's Louise. His description matches how the scene eventually ended up in the film.

"[Louise] starts out to tell him a thing or two. Dissolve out and dissolve in," he explained. "And we find McLintock and Louise gloriously drunk, singing, agreeing, disagreeing, and having a helluva good time. Here Kate [Maureen O'Hara] discovers them. Kate is slightly jealous and greatly humiliated by the fact that McLintock is socializing with the servants."

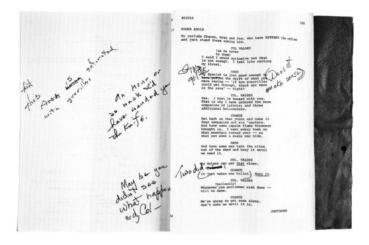

Wayne appreciated other actors who were, like him, deeply dedicated to their craft. In an interview with John Wayne Enterprises, filmmaker Ron Howard reminisced about working with Wayne in his final movie, *The Shootist.* He recalled marveling at Wayne's enthusiasm, saying Wayne was "really into it" during that shoot, despite the fact that Wayne

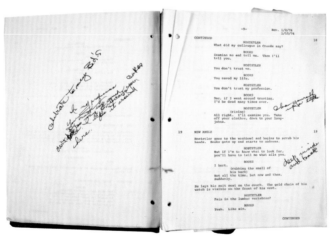

was not in the best of health and his career was winding down. Howard remembers Wayne being glad, and impressed, that a young Howard, then just twenty-one, wanted to rehearse with him during down time. He also reminisced about watching the actor "shape a John Wayne performance" to deliver lines in his signature style, and enjoyed discussing film directing and the lessons Wayne learned from his mentor, John Ford, over the years.

But mostly, Howard says he learned about the art of being a professional from John Wayne—a lesson he carries with him to this day.

I had been on a TV series with Henry Fonda for a couple years, and I think that was useful to me like [The Shootist] was," he says. "They were both from the same era, different kinds of personalities, but they were similar in terms of their button-down professionalism and approach to what they were doing. I think that the thing I really picked up on from him was the idea of simple truths—unsentimental truths being a humanizing quality. On [The Shootist], I saw him applying a sensibility that had endured decades of audience shifts and [was still going strong].

Wayne's interest in Howard wasn't unusual—he admired the young man's dedication. But over the years, some of his casting or crew suggestions seemed designed primarily to help somebody get a break as much as anything else. One example comes from a letter he wrote on August 25, 1965, to his friend Howard Hawks, who was in the middle of prepping *El Dorado,* a 1966 Western starring Wayne and Robert Mitchum. A job was open for someone to play a hired killer, and Wayne proposed John Drew Barrymore, son of the legendary actor. Wayne knew that Barrymore was struggling in that period of his life, and he wanted to help him out.

"[Barrymore] is about as good an actor as we have on the screen," Wayne wrote to Hawks. "Don't you think you should talk to him about playing the professional killer?... I saw him last in Mexico—Puerto Vallarta. I'd heard he was in terrible shape. I kept drinking and thinking about it and drinking and thinking,

and finally decided to go talk to him. By that time I assure you he was in much better shape than I. I saw him again the next day. He looked great physically, but was kind of down in spirits about Hollywood.... I'm quite sure with his background and name you could make some kind of a deal for futures that could be made worthwhile, and give this kid a chance to re-establish himself. I know you are not, and I am not, in the business of philanthropy, but I believe this fellow has something to offer."

Barrymore did not get the role—Hawks already had someone else in mind. But the letter exemplifies Wayne's tendency to offer a hand when he could.

In a June 18, 1964, letter about a business dispute between his company, Batjac, and Paramount Studios, Wayne even took time away from larger contractual issues to try and get one of his loyal employees some work at Paramount. In the letter to executives J. L. Karp and Martin Rackin, he inserted three long paragraphs about the plight of his transportation coordinator, George Coleman.

"In our negotiations some time back, we talked about integrating some of my people from Batjac into Paramount," he wrote. "One of those was George Coleman, who was head

transportation man on *The Alamo, Hondo, High and Mighty* [and other films]. It seems to me his record would recommend him for an occasional job at Paramount, but he has never been hired by them. To further protect this position, I had it put into my contract that Coleman or someone else of my choosing would be put on, if for no other job, than as a driver.... Now, in the [Otto] Preminger picture [*In Harm's Way*], you people not only did not try to get Coleman on as head of transportation, but you informed Preminger's production manager through your lawyer that it would not be necessary for them to use him in any position. I do not know what deal you made with Mr. Preminger, and perhaps Mr. Preminger does not have to hire Coleman, but it is quite obvious there is a breach of my contract if somebody doesn't hire him.... You have put me in a very embarrassing spot with Mr. Preminger.... But someone is going to pay George Coleman from the day this picture starts until the day it finishes, and it isn't going to be Mr. Preminger or Mr. Wayne."

The letter clearly indicates Wayne's passion for protecting his people. He often looked after their interests better than his own, suffering through well-documented financial setbacks over the years due to bad investments by business managers, his messy second divorce, and his need to sink much of his own cash into getting *The Alamo* made (see page 73). Still, regardless of such business entanglements, in most circumstances, his acting work tended to be a cathartic release for John Wayne—the pleasurable part of the business. His archives include letters from Wayne profusely thanking various friends and colleagues for their help and expressing optimism about the success of their labors.

Thank-you notes were, in fact, a Wayne staple following completion of most projects.

"I have just seen *True Grit* for the first time," he wrote Marguerite Roberts, the film's screenwriter, on May 16, 1969. "Actually, I can second quarterback on the cutting, the music, my singing—everything except Marguerite Roberts' work. It was magnificent, and I thank you for your integrity concerning Mr. Portis' book, and for the wonderful ending you devised in his style. Please write once in a while with me in mind."

Roberts appreciated the compliment and wrote him back five days later to say so. She also correctly predicted Wayne's upcoming Academy Award for his performance.

"I had much respect for the Portis novel, and wherever possible I tried to put it on the screen; where it would not play, I did my best to create scenes with the Portis flavor," she wrote him. "I'm pleased you feel I acquitted myself well. At the Director's Guild last night, I saw the film for the first time. My husband had been to a screening a month earlier, and he came home insisting you were a cinch for an Academy nomination; now that I've seen the picture myself, I can only say I agree with him."

The same day he wrote Roberts, Wayne sent similar thank-you notes to Charles Portis, author of the novel on which the movie was based, and to Henry Hathaway, the film's director.

"I saw those wonderful characters come to life because of your writing and [Hathaway's] integrity to your book," he wrote Portis. "I want to say thanks. I'm deeply grateful."

To Hathaway, he wrote not only about the movie but also about their friendship.

"I am deeply grateful for your magnificent direction and integrity to Portis' fine book," he wrote. "This may sound a little stilted, but I'm trying to express a deep feeling of love that I have had for you over the years."

Wayne was close to Hathaway, who directed him in six pictures, including his most honored performance in *True Grit*. But, without question, his closest collaborator was John Ford, who was also his best friend (see page 126). As discussed earlier, Wayne strategically studied Ford's methods early in his career, and it is no secret that is where much of his technical

discipline and desire for control and professionalism on set came from.

"The specific talents that enabled [Ford] to make some truly great pictures are his deep understanding of human nature and his keen sense of the dramatic, as well as comedy," Wayne wrote on January 9, 1973, to a film student, Don Rommereim, who requested information about Ford while writing a college paper on the director's work. "We who have worked in his pictures agree that he is a perfectionist, and because of this is able to obtain excellent performances from each actor, regardless of the type of role."

In addition to working as a member of Ford's crew early in his career (see page 33), as a leading man, Wayne worked for Ford in fourteen movies, and they were in touch throughout their lives on personal and professional levels. In fact, Wayne was always looking for ways to work with his mentor. On August 13, 1954, not long after Wayne had launched his independent production company, Wayne-Fellows, with producer/partner Robert Fellows, he wrote to his friend pitching two stories he had acquired as projects they might be able to work on together. One was based on a magazine article from *True* magazine, called "Cattle Drive to the Yukon," and the other was not named in the letter.

"If you don't like either of these, and even if you do like these, we'll keep looking, because I feel the Wayne-Fellows deal with Warners is about as good as any independent outfit ever

OPPOSITE: *A young Ron Howard with Lauren Bacall and John Wayne in* The Shootist. TOP RIGHT: *Wayne costars with Robert Mitchum in 1966's* El Dorado. PAGES 66–69: *Correspondence between John Wayne and John Ford, longtime director and dear friend.*

Anyway, just between the two of us, General Wedemeyer's outfit, after the election, is interested in backing some pictures. We have some people working on a tax program to check the value of a procedure where we would make pictures without a release. Leo McCarey and Bill Wellman have both come to Bob and me - we did not approach them. I would like to be able to use your name for one picture, if we can set up such a unit and prove its value taxwise. I know you have already said you would do a picture with us, but I wanted you to know what is happening before I bandy your name around.

I hated to move out of the studio, and it's damned irritating. The things that are good at the studio that I have been a party to helping build, like the crews, and the attitude of the crews on pictures - the things that his horrible front office gets, not because they're worth a goddam, but because of the people who make the pictures - these things I hated to leave, and have that smug old bastard sit back and tell me what he had done for me and you and the motion pictures business in general.

I know I can't get any security his way. I see no reason why he should begrudge my doing it another. I guess what I'm trying to say is that I haven't any more room up there for another Yates "Warm Personal Regard".

Enough talk of unpleasantness. How are the English? -- Bless their little pointed heads.

We are working at Cathedral Chapel Church, and your godson just came by and sends his best along with mine.

                    Your Ever Lovin',

Mr. John Ford
c/o MGM Picture   ocation
P.O. Box 950
Nairobi, Kenya
British East Africa

4031 Longridge Avenue
Van Nuys, Calif.
October 29, 1952

Dear Jack,

Are you ruining your life? I hope so. That seems like the
material I would like to ruin my life with.

Regarding my past (and I mean pluperfect past) association
with Republic: As I told you over the phone, Herb called me
in - gave me a friendship kick - and then kicked my teeth out
by saying that his Sales Department was upset, and he was
personally upset, over my going into business for myself -
said that you were against it, and explained to me how
wonderful he had been to me.

As you should know by now, I love the old bastard and have
done many things for him because of that, but he in his own
mind has figured that I did them because of his cunning.

You suggested that I wait a few days before making a decision.
I did wait. I waited long enough to find out he was blabbing in
front of mere acquaintances of his and mine that he had really
told me off. I then set on paper some exact figures, which do
not coincide with his statement regarding the studio's wonderful treatment of me. I enclose copy of my letter and copy of
his answer, which was the reason for my calling a Lambert's
moving van and leaving the studio. He then put out a story that
I had left Republic because he wanted to make "The Alamo" in
Texas and was being loyal to the Texans, and that I insisted on
doing it in Panama. He knows, you know, and I know that the
reason we are not making it in Texas is that he wouldn't put
out the money, and that the reason he caused a hassle at this
time is that he wants to make a picture called "The Golden Tide"
to follow the last abortion he made with Vera; and he also has
another story to follow that, called "Jubilee Trail", which also
happens to be a woman's story. I think I explained that in my
letter to him. I tried to do it in a mannerly fashion - maybe
it wasn't sarcastic enough - I don't know.

sent airmail to: Mr. John Ford
                  Yacht "Araner", Ala Wai Harbor, Honolulu, T. H.

                                              1022 Palm Avenue
                                              Hollywood 46, Calif.
                                              Nov. 28, 1955

Dear Pappy,

First: I think "The Searchers" is just plain wonderful.

I wanted to tell you the other night, or at least before you
got away to Honolulu, what I've decided to do. Here goes.

I built Bob Fellows into such an important character that I
can't do anything with him. I find him incompetent, even
when he's trying. I've encouraged Bob Morrison and Andy
McLaglen and moved them up faster than I should have. I'm
afraid that if I just fired Fellows and moved someone else in,
number one, I'd wreck Fellows' career (what career?) - and
I might have just as many headaches with someone else. So
I'm going to fold the company up. I can make a hell of a deal
at Warners, and an unbelievable one at RKO with Danny O'Shea,
but if I make either one of these deals I couldn't do the Wead
story, so to hell with it. It's more important for me to be
in a picture with you, career-wise - for my health - and for
my mental relief.

So I'm going to let Charlie Feldman talk to Loew, who is the
guy behind the guns at MGM now, to set the deal, and if you
hear I haven't talked to Schary or Thau, don't think that I'm
ducking the picture -- it's just that Feldman can make a
better deal with Loew.

Back to "The Searchers" - I don't think the music is great,
but I think it's all right. At first I had hoped it would be a
little nostalgic, but the whole treatment is so different than
the usual Western, that I think this music is probably more
appropriate. It's just a wonderful picture. You got great
performances out of everyone, and it has a raw brutalness
without any pettiness or meanness.

All I can say is - Thanks again, Coach.

                                      Your everloving,

JOHN FORD

November 4th, 1957

Dear Duke,

Lo. I'm back. Weary. I miss you, but not as much as
I miss Web. My hair is down my back. However, it's
nice to be back.

I have not seen HIM yet. HE has not called. I don't
expect him to.

By now I know you're busy on the picture and I wish both
you and Johnny Huston a lot of luck.

Incidentally, I became quite friendly with Kurosawa, the
great Japanese director. He is a great admirer of "ours",
and would like to have the pleasure of visiting you while
you are in Tokyo. He is a terribly, terribly nice guy.

If you see any beautiful Japanese dolls - not babes - dolls -
I wish you'd get a couple for Barbara. I owe her several.
The last lot went astray. But never mind any samurai swords.

Do you enjoy beer? I do.

Thanks a lot for the books on the Civil War. They're
terrific.

Lots of love,

Coach.

P.S. Would you like to do a Western sometime?

times, and don't get sunstroke. I know, because I spent a winter once on the North African coast.

I'm working very hard preparing for "The Last Hurrah". Also trying to get the Irish picture shown. Also cutting the submarine story, besides working on "Judge And His Hangman".

Despite union troubles, they tell me that Rome is a good place to make pictures. I don't know - perhaps Vienna is better, but the lakes around Como and Lago Maggiore are beautiful.

Pilar was over to the house for dinner the other night and we had a swell time. Charlie Schnee and his wife were there, and we played all the games: Coat, I Took A Trip, the Card Reading trick, and finally called up the card shark, who turned out to be a foreign lady by the name of Josephine Saenz. Charlie and his wife went crazy - completely mystified.

Well, give my love to everybody. I hope there are some equestrian statutes in Ghadames, or at least a few Arab horses, so that we may add to our valuable collection of Bondiana.

If you meet some nice Arab that you are particularly fond of, why don't you bring him back, and we'll run him for the Mayor of Beverly Hills. Look what they're doing in Dublin.

I will now finish, again wishing you all the best and much affection, and proceed to make a pass at Mary St. John.

As ever,

Jack

Pass completed.

Jan. 25, 1957

Dear Duke,

Your letter and wire regarding "Hangman" and Hecht-Lancaster
arrived the same day. Gawd, that's some mail system the Arabs
have. Could be by camel back. Might be a good idea if they dug
up Mussolini again.

Regarding the Hecht-Lancaster deal, it is just one of those things.
They're interested in it and they asked me about it. Natch, I made
no commitments. Remember, this is Jack speaking, and you're
Duke. You're the guy that makes commitments - at bars, lunch
tables, steam baths, airplanes, George V Hotel, at Batjac, at
Romanoff's - oh, hell, the list is too long. You got the cast twisted.
If you have made some sort of an arrangement or have had a
preliminary chat with U.A., that's okay with me. Hecht-Lancaster
have never done me any favors. It's one of those Bolton-MCA
ideas, so forget it. How about Republic? (Time out while Mary
St. John goes and throws up.)

Had a wonderful press preview of "Wings Of Eagles" (Gawd, what
a title) aboard the carrier Lexington last night. The Navy really
put on a great show for us, dinner inspection, the works. The
picture went over great. The bluejackets were with it every
minute, and during the dramatic moments there was complete
silence in that great big hangar deck, which, as you know, is
bigger than St. Peter's. Check with Terry Wilson and Chuck
Hayward. They know the size, qualifications, height, width and
everything about St. Peter's. If they are busy making passes at
your wop leading woman, ask Web Overlander, the Barber of
Seville.

So you got yourself tied up with a new gimmick. It all sounds
great, but how's the story?

We - Barbara, Ken, Maizie, Butt Ward, and Mary, are going
to your house tomorrow night to see the "Bob Mathias Story".
Also "Rio Grande" - my favorite picture. Bob Mathias and his
wife, of course, will be there.

It is very, very cold here. Gawd, I envy you out on that hot,
sultry, dry desert. Be very careful and wear your hat at all

1022 PALM AVENUE   HOLLYWOOD 46, CALIFORNIA   CRESTVIEW 5-6175

Dear Duke =

Now hear this #

We (cohn ford etc) made
tentative arrangements with
Orson Wells - an actor of repute =
+ some disrepute - to play the
part of Skeffington in Sast
Hurrah' # This bit of news
was distributed to the Press -

The following morning Mr
Cohn + Mr Kahane received on
their desks (a messenger service)

OVER

a huge pile of documents -
about Wells Communistic or Sub-
versive activities (alleged)

These were sent by an
actor who had said all over town
that he was to play the part.
a Ward Bond #

Now I know Ward Bond
very well- in fact he has dined at
my home = he knows my family +
all of that = in fact - in a small
measure I helped him in his
career #

But Ward Bond did

not come to one+ protest about
Wells prochvities - (alleged) No!
He must go to Colu+ Kahane *

You know, my very decided
views on Traitors. Commies. fellow
travelers + Such like = you also
know my integrity in making films*
also my ideas of justice. you
are not guilty until proven so.
(and the Jury is not necessarily
Wad Bond) Whady think
of it? I cant get mad.

its so ridiculous — from now
its not the "Star Spangled Banner"
but Wards new-coat —

Strangely enuff — if the great
American W.B — cant play the
play. He thinks Spencer Tracy
would do = what modesty! Tracy=
now — if you want a record!!

Now I am without a favorite
shirt# please come back #

_____

I may still make a quick
trip to Rome= as this thing here
is all screwed up. no decisions.
Cohns criticisms of the script
moronic = etc etc etc

also- tell Web my hair's
down my back (no cracks)
give my love to Pilar.

have you given any thoughts
to "Hangman"?

do you love Ward Bond?

much affection

P.S. Since writing- I had a date
with O. Wells- 1 p.m. Sat. He
didn't show & at 1.45 PM his
Secretary called- the dear

Boy had a slight fever -
upset etc #
      So fuck him -

         Coach -

      fuck Bond - too

"I SAW THOSE WONDERFUL CHARACTERS COME TO LIFE BECAUSE OF
YOUR WRITING AND [HATHAWAY'S] INTEGRITY TO YOUR BOOK," HE WROTE PORTIS.
"I WANT TO SAY THANKS. I'M DEEPLY GRATEFUL."

had," he wrote Ford. "And if you join with us in a picture you can be assured that the distributing company won't be taking it all away from us in percentages for overhead, percentages for distribution, and percentages you never heard of, plus checking costs, phony advertising costs, taxes and what-not; and besides that, all the best crew that Republic ever had is over here to make it easy and to make it fun to make pictures."

After that letter, Wayne made four more pictures with Ford, including one of their greatest collaborations, *The Searchers*, two years later.

Not all of Wayne's filmmaking experiences were as positive as *The Searchers* or *True Grit*, however. There are stories of projects that were difficult to launch or execute and business disputes delaying certain movies. Also, filmmakers occasionally rubbed Wayne the wrong way for various reasons, such as John Huston on *The Barbarian and the Geisha* (see page 74) and Frank Capra on 1964's *Circus World*. On the latter, Wayne's loyalty to writer and friend James Grant, and to Grant's version of the story, caused Capra to leave the project; he was replaced with Henry Hathaway.

None of those stories match his twenty-year fight to get *The Alamo* made—an epic struggle that Wayne waged relentlessly until he finally achieved his goal. The movie was deeply important to Wayne, and issues over financing and control of the project eventually led him to end his longtime relationship with

71

Republic Pictures. Years later, Wayne made the movie himself from scratch (see page 73).

"For me, [the motion-picture business] is the career that I'm dependent upon to make my fortune," he wrote Republic studio chief Herbert Yates on August 20, 1951, as their relationship was falling apart over the project's fate. "It's no plaything to me. It's my livelihood. I'm very interested in it and take pride in accomplishment."

Such words illustrate the seriousness of the matter for Wayne, who felt, with good reason, that he had played a significant role in building Republic as a studio and that, as he wrote in some letters, Yates had "double-crossed" him over the years. His argument with Yates began well before he left Republic over *The Alamo*. As early as 1946, in a letter dated May 2, he wrote Yates to protest abhorrent conditions that met the cast and crew of *Angel and the Badman* in Arizona.

"I do not consider this [to be] fair cooperation in getting the best out of the people," he wrote Yates. "It is just as important to have reasonable comforts for the crew to have their meals and for the principals to relax between scenes and rehearse as it is to build a set."

TOP: *John Wayne on the set of* The Searchers. *Front row, left to right: director John Ford, Dorothy Jordan, and back row, left to right: actors Jack Pennick and Jeffrey Hunter.* ABOVE: *Aissa Wayne rides a baby elephant on the set of* Hatari! *During filming, Wayne insisted on playing the stunt scenes himself. He and other actors and crew actually corralled the animals in sequences engineered by director Howard Hawks—a practice no longer permitted today.*

John Wayne's single-minded pursuit to make *The Alamo* lasted twenty years. Eventually, to finance the film, he became an independent producer and hooked up with United Artists and a consortium of Texas oilmen, with Wayne himself funding the balance. Among the oilmen was Texas billionaire Clint Murchison, who would later find fame as the original owner of the Dallas Cowboys football team. When Murchison stepped into the breach, he found everlasting gratitude from John Wayne, who addressed his letters to Murchison, "Dear Boss."

"Regarding our venture, I know how tight money is," he wrote Murchison on October 3, 1959, while the movie was in production. "I can't tell you how much I appreciate your backing up your word, though there were many reasonable excuses you could have used to back out."

He added in another letter to Murchison on June 10, 1960, a few months before the movie's release, "I really appreciate what you did for me, and want you to know it had a lot to do with the integrity and hard work that went into the picture. I couldn't let such confidence down. It may sound a little stilted, but I really mean it."

At the end of the day, Wayne never personally made any money on *The Alamo*. Its performance allowed United Artists to profit and Wayne to pay back Murchison and his colleagues, but there was little to nothing left over to recoup Wayne's own investment. But then, his primary investment wasn't financial, as his son Patrick, who costarred in the film, points out.

"He never gave up on it," Patrick says today. "He started on it when he was a fledgling producer at Republic in the 1940s, and it took twenty years for it to reach fruition. For him, the story of the Alamo represented everything that is great about this country. He always said that nowhere else in the world could he have had the kind of success he ended up having, and he wanted to pay homage to that, and to this country, through this movie, and that is exactly what he did."

In costume, John Wayne directs a scene from The Alamo—*a movie he worked decades to get made.*

John Wayne and Eiko Ando in The Barbarian and the Geisha, *1958.*

THE BARBARIAN

Despite periodic battles over the years with studios and critics over projects like *The Alamo* and *The Green Berets*, John Wayne was traditionally upbeat about the projects he worked on. One film, however, crops up repeatedly in his archives as possibly the most difficult of his lengthy career.

That movie was *The Barbarian and the Geisha*, shot in Japan in 1958—a lengthy project with a script Wayne found unsatisfying and a testy collaboration with director John Huston, whose methods were an anathema to Wayne after years in the John Ford school of filmmaking. Much has been written about their disagreements on the film, which was a box-office bust. However, in journalist Wayne Warga's papers sits an entire unpublished chapter of Wayne's never-finished autobiography devoted to the pain of the project. Warga wrote that Wayne placed the failure of the movie "squarely on the director, John Huston." Wayne loved the chapter, but he told Warga not to include it in any finished book.

Warga wrote that Wayne told him, "If there is one person out there who will accuse me of being petty by writing something like this, I've done the wrong thing. Huston's career speaks for itself. He has to live with it."

The unpublished chapter reveals Wayne's thoughts while finishing the picture—in a scene on horseback with direction from Huston that, once again, in his view, was unsatisfactory.

"I had, for a number of years, blamed Gregory Peck—an otherwise excellent actor—for his bad performance as Ahab in *Moby Dick*," Wayne wrote. "I had desperately wanted that part and was annoyed with Peck's portrayal. I remembered this, sitting on my horse waiting for the cameras to roll, and realized what kind of picture and performance this was going to be. Probably worse than Peck's as Ahab. The director of *Moby Dick* was John Huston and I finally realized Peck didn't have a chance. Nor, for that matter, did I."

TOP LEFT: *John and Patrick Wayne on the set of* McLintock! *in 1963. Wayne religiously played chess on set with cast, crew, and friends whenever time permitted.* BOTTOM RIGHT: *John Wayne with John Ford and Jimmy Stewart on the set of* The Man Who Shot Liberty Valance.

In 1951, his frustration grew as he perceived Yates interfering with the strategic plan Wayne had made to produce *Bullfighter and the Lady,* which Wayne spearheaded as a vehicle starring Robert Stack. He sent Yates a detailed three-page letter in January 1951 reviewing their understanding and how important it was to Wayne to produce the film himself. Yates originally took Wayne's name off the picture as a producer (Wayne later got it restored) without even talking to Wayne.

"If ever a picture should be called a John Wayne Production, this is it," he wrote. "It is, therefore, damned irritating to not be given even the courtesy of a call when it was time to figure out the credit titles for the picture.... I have mixed emotions of being hurt, and mad, and goddamned disappointed."

By that summer, *The Alamo* was in process, first as a coproduction between Wayne and Republic, as he had originally arranged, and then it was taken over by Republic on Yates's insistence, arbitrarily in Wayne's view, and the production was moved out of Mexico where Wayne had set it up. In an August 20, 1951, letter to Yates, Wayne made it clear he'd had enough.

"I repeat I am not going to work my butt off for this studio and be belittled and argued with when I am doing something, and then have it turn out well, and not even so goddamned much as be thanked," he wrote in the four-page missive. "This happened on the *Bullfighter and the Lady.* I am not going to plan a picture, work and worry my head off, to have it stopped because you have made up your mind—without looking into the facts—what should be done.

"I've spent the last two weeks with my head buzzing with a lot of negative thinking that would have been unnecessary had you not double-crossed me. I can't spend all my time at this studio fighting with people who do not understand or recognize the needs of Class A pictures. I have my health to think of, and so I repeat I know you like me very much, but you have not appreciated or understood the hard work I have put in for this studio, and I am not going to do it anymore until I am certain everyone is behind me…. Perhaps we can make it next October. All I know is that I am not up to the worry and pressure it would take to get it under way now. I've left my fight in the locker room."

Shortly after that letter, Wayne and Yates had a famous argument at the Republic Pictures' offices, and he and secretary Mary St. John stormed out, never to return. Republic, however, owned the original *Alamo* script and turned it into a 1955 picture called *The Last Command*. Eventually, Wayne would start over, producing, financing, directing, and starring in the film some eight years later in 1960 (see page 73).

In an October 29, 1952, letter to John Ford, who had his own battles with Republic, Wayne elaborated on why the breakup was necessary. In the letter, it's clear how agonizing the incident was for John Wayne.

"I hated to move out of the studio, and it's damned irritating," he wrote. "The things that are good at the studio that I have been a party to helping build, like the crews, and the attitude of the crews on pictures—the things that this horrible front office gets, not because they're worth a goddamn, but because of the people who make the pictures—these things I hated to leave."

Despite such painful trials, the portrait that emerges of Wayne on set—as a colleague and collaborator as described by those who worked with him regularly and knew him best—is that he was unpretentious, friendly with crew members at all levels, respectful of craftspeople, loyal to his closest associates to a fault, rigidly disciplined as an actor, and during downtime, an enthusiastic practical joker.

Terry Leonard was an athlete at the University of Arizona whose Olympic aspirations were derailed by injuries, but he eventually developed a career as a stuntman in Hollywood. He started with some brief, uncredited work on *McLintock!* in 1963, and then on *El Dorado* (1966), *Rio Lobo* (1970), *Big Jake* (1971), and *The Train Robbers* (1973). He credits Wayne and his team with helping him break in and learn the ropes, particularly the three famous stuntmen who worked closest with John Wayne— Yakima Canutt, Dean Smith, and Chuck Roberson, Leonard's mentor who first introduced him to Wayne.

Wayne told Leonard early on to call him "Duke" and soon began inviting the greenhorn into his card games.

"I learned to play hearts on the set of *Rio Lobo* down in Mexico—it was the first set I worked as a full-fledged Hollywood stuntman," Leonard recalls. "Wayne was a hell of a card player and great at chess and poker. I was invited to play with him, Chuck Roberson, and Dean Smith. I kept losing and losing. But if John Wayne was down, he had a signal to the [second assistant director]. They would call him and say they were ready for him on set, and if we were playing, he had to stop and go. This guy would watch for his signal, and if Duke was losing the hand, which was very seldom, he 'had to go' and we all dropped our hands. I lost all my per diem learning to play hearts with those guys."

Observers who visited Wayne on set also emphasize his fondness for child actors and their fondness for him. In a chapter of his never-finished biography manuscript, writer Wayne Warga described watching Wayne "spend hours teaching the boys how to fake their punches and angles for film" during production of *The Cowboys*. A year later, in a *National Review* article in April 1973, writer Lorraine Gauguin wrote about spending time with Wayne on the set of *Cahill, United States Marshal* in one of his favorite locations, Durango, Mexico. In a draft of the article found in the Wayne archives, she talks about being interrupted by one of Wayne's young costars in the film, a child actor named Clay O'Brien, who played one of his sons.

She describes Wayne handing the boy some taffy and the youngster suddenly losing a tooth when he bit into it. Clay was immediately worried that a gap in his mouth would not match with footage already shot.

"Now, now, they'll drive you into Durango and we'll have a dentist put in a fake tooth and you'll be able to work tomorrow," she reported that Wayne said in an attempt to comfort the youngster.

And, of course, there was the joy Wayne experienced filming *Big Jake* in 1971 with his sons Patrick and Ethan. Ethan was only nine and making his acting debut. He rarely gave detailed advice, but when he did, it tended to be simple and straightforward.

"Good acting is reacting," he told Warga in 1969. "The minute a person has to act on the screen, something is wrong. Actually, though, reacting is acting. Better to have one look that works than to say 20 lines." ✪

MEMORABLE MUGS

In the early 1950s, John Wayne began a tradition of making specially engraved coffee mugs for all crew and cast members on each of his projects. According to journalist Wayne Warga's interview in 1971 with Mary St. John, the tradition began in 1951 with *Flying Leathernecks*. The ceramic mugs with specially engraved images and messages became treasured possessions for anyone who worked on a Wayne movie.

"I have four of the mugs on my mantle right now," states stuntman Terry Leonard, who indeed worked on four John Wayne pictures. "I had them specially hooked up to the bottom of my mantle so that even if there is an earthquake, they won't fall. I want them to survive even if nothing else does."

In fact, production and distribution of those cups was a major job that Wayne typically entrusted to Mary St. John. During production of *The Sons of Katie Elder* in 1965, for instance, she typed up a list of seventy people for whom she would have to get mugs produced, plus four more for family members, with special instructions from Wayne about what to write on each cup. In the Wayne archives' folder from that project are original sketches Wayne commissioned from a local artist to be transformed into a logo for all those mugs. Dozens of thank-you notes from appreciative crewmembers are also preserved in the archives from that movie, and also for the mugs handed out after production on 1963's *Donovan's Reef,* among other films.

CHAPTER FIVE

MAN
IN
UNIFORM

"THE WEEKS AND MONTHS I SPENT IN VIETNAM AND AT FORT
BENNING FILMING THE PICTURE *THE GREEN BERETS*, AND
WORKING WITH MANY GREEN BERET TRAINEES AND VETERANS,
BROUGHT ME VERY CLOSE TO THEM. THEY, LIKE YOUR SON,
ARE MEN OF WHOM ALL OF US SHOULD BE VERY PROUD.
THANK YOU FOR WRITING ME ABOUT YOUR SON. WHAT YOU
HAVE TOLD ME ABOUT HIM FURTHER CONFIRMS MY HIGH
REGARD FOR OUR FIGHTING MEN."

—JOHN WAYNE, IN A FEBRUARY 22, 1968 LETTER OF CONDOLENCE TO THE
FAMILY OF A SPECIAL FORCES MEMBER KILLED IN ACTION IN VIETNAM

I T WAS THE TYPE OF HONOR THAT REGULARLY CAME JOHN WAYNE'S WAY. A Texas chapter of the national veterans service organization known as AMVETS wrote him in September 1975 asking permission to name AMVETS Post 57 in Fort Worth, Texas, after him. They cited his years of service to those who served in the armed forces.

On October 2, 1975, Wayne, though honored, declined for fairly perfunctory reasons—he wasn't a veteran.

"I am most complimented by your offer; but since I was not a member of the Armed Forces, I do not feel that it is a proper gesture for me to accept," he wrote, sending along his compliments.

The issue of Wayne's lack of service in the US Armed Forces during World War II has been debated for years, since he rose to be a symbol of the American fighting man in so many movies and was so outspoken on military issues. Critics accused him of being a hawk with no experience in combat. There are no personal letters or communications in the Wayne archives that directly address this matter in Wayne's own words. But what is known has been well documented: as a youth, he had hoped to

attend the US Naval Academy and become a career naval officer, but he was not accepted and went to USC instead. Then, by the time the United States entered World War II, he was married and the father of four children with a legitimate 3-A (family dependency) draft exemption. However, he also wrote his mentor and friend John Ford a couple of times to no avail about finding ways to join Ford's unit during the war. In the early 2000s, a document surfaced in the National Archives signed by Wayne that suggests he attempted, at one point, to join the photo unit of the Office of Strategic Services (OSS)—precursor to the CIA—in 1943. Additionally, when his draft status changed to make him eligible for service, there is also documentation that Republic Pictures wrote the Selective Service Department to urge that

Wayne's draft eligible status be deferred, since he was under contract to the studio at the time.

In a July 16, 1969, letter, Wayne defended his alleged lack of experience in war zones. Retired Marine Corps Major Eugene A. McNerney had written to Wayne criticizing him for using active military equipment during filming of *The Green Berets,* and needling him over his lack of official military service. Wayne's response made clear that he had, in fact, risked his personal safety over the years out of a desire to visit the troops.

"For your information, I have been shot at in anger at Finschhafen, New Guinea, and Arawe, New Britain, during World War II, and at Chu Lai in [the Vietnam War]—and in 1966 I visited every 'A' camp of the Green Berets, where they were getting shot at more than once a day," he defiantly wrote Major McNerney.

Still, none of the letters in the present-day Wayne archives details specifically why he never joined the military; today, despite various accounts in various biographies, the exact details are probably lost to the sands of time. What is clear, however, is that Wayne's participation in movies that promoted the armed forces, his numerous positive portrayals of the American fighting man, his USO service, and his interest in the troops and support of the Vietnam War were contributions that are respected and appreciated by veterans' organizations and military institutions to this day.

Throughout his life, Wayne was consistently committed to supporting and honoring the troops. He greatly admired those who served in the armed forces, and that affection was largely returned in kind.

In an August 26, 1965, letter to theatrical agent Jules Sherr, who was trying to arrange a USO tour of celebrities to Vietnam, Wayne casually mentioned that he had participated in such tours during World War II. He gave Sherr some advice about how to organize it, but then said he would have to wait to participate—he was still recuperating from his 1964 cancer surgery and his doctors advised him to hold off. He eventually participated in multiple USO tours during the Vietnam War, and his experiences during the conflict seemed to make Wayne genuinely introspective, on a personal level, about the sacrifices of military personnel, if his 1970s-era letters are any indication.

Indeed, the archives are filled with letters inviting Wayne to various military events or activities, or thanking him for his participation and offering him honors on behalf of various groups. After his tour of Vietnam in 1966 in preparation for making *The Green Berets,* for instance, the Department of Defense presented

PAGE 78: *In uniform for* The Green Berets. OPPOSITE: *John Wayne on a visit to Vietnam in 1966. Private First Class Fonsell Wofford, 3rd Battalion, 7th Marines, gets an autograph on his helmet.* TOP RIGHT: *A rescue scene on a Normandy beach during filming of 1962's* The Longest Day. *Wayne only had a cameo on that star-studded picture.* BOTTOM RIGHT: *Wayne plays a scene as Lt. Colonel Jim Shannon in* Jet Pilot.

GREEN BERETS: NO BACKING DOWN

The Green Berets was one of two passion projects that John Wayne personally labored to finance, direct, and get made despite significant obstacles. The other, of course, was *The Alamo* in 1960 (see page 73). Wayne admitted that he hoped *The Green Berets* would help improve the image of the Vietnam War effort, and he never wavered in this goal even as the project garnered significant criticism, far beyond what he had anticipated, in the troubled year of 1968.

Why did he push on? "Well, he was never one to back down," his son Patrick Wayne, who costarred in the film, says today. "It was the same kind of drive he showed when trying to make *The Alamo,* but obviously different context. We were in the middle of a contentious war, the country was polarized, and it was very emotional. Most of the reactions were emotional. And so, they were lashing out at him and the film from an emotional place. But he wouldn't budge from his position—these were American fighting men, he was proud of them, and he wanted to show them in the best light. He felt we were at war—right or wrong, good or bad, they were fighting on our behalf, and we should support them. They were sent there, after all, so he felt you don't turn your back on them."

But, Patrick adds, "the backlash did get out of hand. However, the odd thing is that it raised such a furor in the public eye that the conversation got into the news section of the newspapers, not just the entertainment section. And that meant the movie got a lot of exposure. In the end, what happened was that many more people went to see it. This particular movie got more than his traditional audience to show up, and he was always proud of that."

Indeed, sitting in a box in the John Wayne archives is a clipping of an original negative review of the film by famed film critic Richard Schickel. Using a Sharpie pen, John Wayne wrote over text of the review, "6½ million in three weeks, thanks to the left-wing overkill."

Like The Alamo, The Green Berets *was a passion project for John Wayne.* LEFT: *Wayne directs a sequence during filming.* ABOVE: *The negative review of the movie that Wayne kept in his files—writing over it a defiant statement about how successful it was at the box office.*

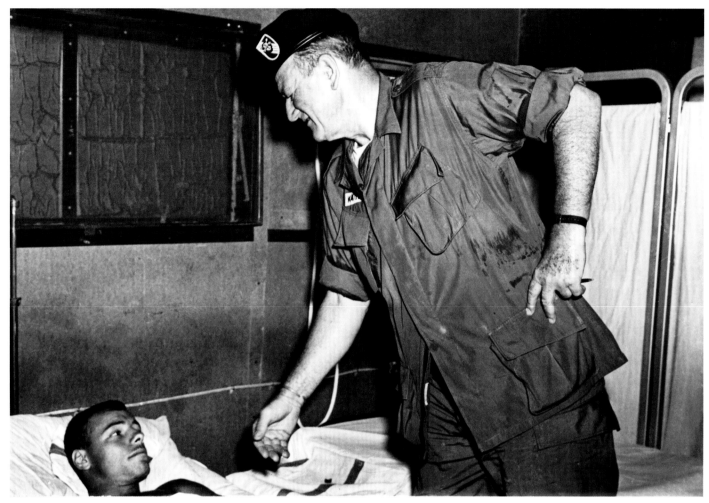

Wayne with its Defense Certificate of Esteem. When he wrote Stanley Resor, then secretary of the army, to thank him for the award, it was quite clear that Wayne was more excited about the opportunity to meet soldiers in Vietnam than about the award itself.

"The friendly looks, the friendly words, the friendly jibes and laughter from those dedicated men in Vietnam are the greatest reward a man can have to store up with his fondest memories," Wayne wrote to Secretary Resor.

After Western movies, John Wayne was most known for and enjoyed the military genre. He played, at one time or another, a member of virtually every branch of the military, including, in crossing genres, a member of the US Cavalry in several Westerns. He performed in eighteen war pictures (see list on page 92) playing active fighting men in major conflicts, and he also played a photojournalist in a war zone in the 1937 picture *I Cover the War.* Among his war pictures are some of his classics, like *The Fighting Seabees* (1944), *They Were Expendable* (1945), *Sands of Iwo Jima* (1949), *Flying Leathernecks* (1951),

TOP: *John Wayne visits with a wounded American soldier in the hospital while in uniform during filming of* The Green Berets *during the Vietnam conflict.* BOTTOM RIGHT: *An authentic beret Wayne wore in* The Green Berets *and a doughboy style helmet from* Back to Bataan, *from Wayne's personal collection.*

The Longest Day (1962), and *In Harm's Way* (1965). That list also includes his most controversial film, which he starred in and directed at the height of the Vietnam conflict, *The Green Berets* (1968).

Over the years, Wayne developed close contacts and relationships with the military, and he occasionally interacted directly with various branches or government agencies while researching or producing particular films. In 1956, Wayne wrote a friend, retired General Clarence A. Shoop, then a vice president of the Hughes Aircraft Company, asking for help in arranging military logistical support for a remote location in Libya for filming 1957's *Legend of the Lost*.

Shoop, who served periodically as a technical adviser on war pictures for Wayne and others, promptly dashed off letters to officials at Wheelus Air Force Base in Tripoli requesting they assist filmmakers in providing food, a helicopter, and staff members to help location managers acquire materials in Libya. Air Force Colonel William J. Cain Jr. immediately wrote Shoop back, agreeing to offer as much assistance to Wayne as possible, largely because of "his past assistance to the Air Force," but also, it appears, because of his obvious star power.

"We look forward to having [costar Sophia Loren] and Mr. Wayne appear on the base, should they desire to do so," Colonel Cain wrote to General Shoop on December 28, 1956. "I am sure they will both be more than welcome in the Officer's Mess."

In 1964, Wayne also filmed on board the USS *Kearsarge* antisubmarine naval vessel during the making of *In Harm's Way*. Wayne spent time living on the vessel, socializing with the crew, and studying navy procedures.

OPPOSITE: *John Wayne happily greets American soldiers during his tour of Vietnam in 1966.* INSET: *Wayne poses with South Vietnamese troops.*

Without question, Wayne's 1966 tour of Vietnam and the subsequent events surrounding the making of *The Green Berets* deeply impacted him. In developing the project, he worked closely with the US Department of Defense and the Johnson White House despite their obvious overall political differences. As the war escalated, Wayne admitted that he wanted *The Green Berets* to be a vehicle for rallying support for American troops at a time when antiwar sentiment was growing. He walked a fine line in planning the project, between his oft-stated belief that such pictures should be entertainment vehicles first and foremost and his belief that he should assist in boosting the war effort.

In fact, he said just that in a letter he wrote as he was developing the picture on February 18, 1966, to Bill Moyers, who would go on to become a major television correspondent but at the time was serving as special assistant to President Johnson.

"We are confident that the finished script will be one that adheres closely to the thinking of President Johnson and the whole Administration regarding the role being played by the U.S. fighting men in Vietnam," he wrote to Moyers. He also talked in the letter about wanting "to enlighten" the American people about the ruthlessness of the North Vietnamese enemy, and he gave

some specific examples of how he wanted to do that in the film. He closed by expressing confidence that "these are the types of things we can insert in the picture without it becoming a message vehicle or interfering with the entertainment."

When he visited South Vietnam in the summer of 1966, Wayne was given a silver friendship bracelet from the Montagnard Strike Force unit (made up of indigenous Vietnamese

John Wayne spent time with officers and enlisted men alike during his 1966 tour of Vietnam. INSET: Posing with sailors. OPPOSITE, TOP: Officers escort Wayne during the course of his visit. OPPOSITE, BOTTOM: As this image illustrates, Wayne clearly enjoyed hanging out with American GIs that year while spending time at the former Binh Thuy Air Base in Vietnam.

people) of the US Army Special Forces—a bracelet he wore the rest of his life. "It was given to him as a token of brotherhood by the Montagnards while Mr. Wayne was making a tour of Vietnam in 1966," his longtime secretary, Mary St. John, explained in the *Phoenix Gazette* in June 1970. "It was bent to fit his wrist and he has never taken it off." That same month, Wayne mentioned the bracelet in a letter to Captain Richard D. Bishop of the US Army Special Forces, writing, "you can tell my friends I am proud to wear it."

Wayne also ended up with a Chicom carbine rifle presented to him by American troops in the field on June 23, 1966. According to an accompanying letter, the rifle was "part of the large cache of weapons and ammunition taken from a Communist ship captured at the mouth of the Co Chien River on 20 June 1966. Please accept the weapon as a token of our appreciation for your visit today and the many hours of enjoyment you have given us all at the cinema."

The letter was signed by dozens of GIs, and indeed, one of the interesting things about Wayne's visit to see the troops in 1966 was the personal impact it had on individual soldiers who wrote him following the visit. Often, they addressed their letters to "Duke," as if they were close friends. From General William Westmoreland down to the average grunt in the field, Wayne tried hard to answer these notes with appreciative letters of his own in the weeks and months following his trip.

He wrote Brigadier General Joseph W. Stilwell on April 18, 1966, to thank him for arranging a visit to Fort Bragg, North Carolina, to watch Special Forces training firsthand. Wayne told General Stilwell that, in his view, after watching the soldiers train, "the reaction is that these men would give every American a more generous heart."

He also quoted poet Stephen Vincent Benét in the note, declaring the virtues of patriotism: "Now for my country that it

may still live, All that I have, all that I am I'll give. It is not much beside the gift of the brave. And yet accept it since 'tis all I have."

When Air Force Captain Robert S. Neilson and Special Forces Group Captain B. C. Burgoyne both wrote shortly after his trip, sending Wayne photos of himself with troops in the field

for him to autograph, he wrote them back (signing the photos, of course) and paid homage to the troops.

"I can't tell you how proud I am to know each and every man I met in Vietnam," he wrote to Neilson on August 4, 1966. "I wish I could let them know how thankful I am to them for their unswerving dedication."

That same day, he sent Burgoyne a note informing him of the "healthy respect" he had gained for Burgoyne's unit—the

TOP LEFT: *John Wayne performs a scene from* Sands of Iwo Jima. TOP RIGHT: *Wayne stands next to a plaque bearing the Marine Corps. emblem.* BOTTOM: *Wayne in* In Harm's Way.

There are many examples of the esteem American servicemen had for John Wayne, who always returned that esteem in kind. One particularly memorable episode involved the USS *Pueblo*, which in January 1968 was seized by North Korea for allegedly spying within its territorial waters and its crew taken captive. The world watched mesmerized as events unfolded over the next eleven months.

During their captivity, the *Pueblo* crew and officers experienced threats, torture, and humiliations that ultimately led their commander, Lloyd Mark "Pete" Bucher, to sign a "confession" on behalf of the crew—a document he later rescinded and disavowed, but which Bucher said he signed in order to prevent the execution of some of his men. That document allowed North Korea to save face while freeing the crew and avoiding a larger confrontation with the United States.

Upon their return home to San Diego in late December 1968, it was decided to throw the returnees a small party. Bucher himself sent John Wayne a telegram inviting him to the party specifically "because of your constant stand for America and her servicemen."

Wayne not only attended, he decided to pay for the affair and presented awards to returning crew members, despite the swirling controversy over Bucher's actions and the so-called confession. It was a happy night, one that Wayne was proud to participate in, and from that moment onward, he became keenly interested in the crew's welfare. In early 1969, Bucher wrote him a long letter, thanking him for his kindness in "celebrating our return" and filling Wayne in on events involving the official navy inquiry into the affair.

Wayne continued to stay in touch with Bucher, and he remained concerned how "politicians" might end up handling the returning *Pueblo* crew. Even before Bucher's 1969 letter, Wayne sent a telegram to Secretary of Defense Melvin Laird on January 23, 1969, in which he pleaded with the secretary to make sure that Commander Bucher would not "be made the scapegoat of either the Navy's or the last Administration's mistakes or lack of positive action at the time of the capture of the *Pueblo*. [Bucher]

and his crew are only a month removed from a year of bestial torture. I pray that he is not ill-used by politicians, either in or out of the service."

A few days later, he got a quick reply from J.B. Colwell, vice admiral of the US Navy, assuring him that the rights of the crew were being protected and explaining how the tribunal would work. At the end of the day, a recommendation of court martial was issued against Bucher, but Secretary of the Navy John Chafee overruled it. Bucher continued his navy career, and he and his crew were finally granted prisoner-of-war medals in 1989.

USS PUEBLO
AGER-2

2401 Neoma Street
San Diego, Calif.
February 26, 1969

Dear Mr. & Mrs. Wayne:

It troubles me that I have taken so long to express the deep gratitude and appreciation that we of PUEBLO felt when you so kindly troubled yourselves to help celebrate our return to God's country.

We have been busy here with the Court of Inquiry which continues to drag on. My fervent hope is that the complete truth of the "Pueblo incident" will be brought to light through the offices of these proceedings and that the future episodes of this sort will be prevented, or if they do happen lets hope to God that the Administration has the guts to handle it in the only language those animals understand.

Rose was so absolutely thrilled to have had the opportunity to meet both of you. Your very appropriate comment regarding her courage and poise made me indeed proud.

Mr. Wayne, you are indeed among the greatest patriots this country has ever been fortunate enough to have. Thank God for you, sir, and may you continue to enjoy the tremendous success you have always had in your profession.

We learned with regret of the accident you suffered on location in Durango and pray that it will respond quickly to treatment and rest.

Rose is including three photos taken when you were here. Two are for you and the other she would appreciate your autograph on. A self-addressed, self-stamped envelope is enclosed for your convenience.

Mrs. Wayne, we do of course remember your kind invitation to visit with you and your husband some weekend. What I would, of course, enjoy would be a chance to see your boat or even have a chance to conn her. In any event, we most certainly will accept your generous offer at your convenience when and if this damn investigation ends.

Most sincerely,

Pete Bucher

5th Special Forces Group—during his trip. He also quoted—as he did in a few other letters to different people—General Curtis LeMay's famous comment about honor and the military. The fighting men he met, he told Burgoyne, were precisely "the kind of fellows LeMay wrote about" when he said:

> *I hope that the United States of America has not yet passed the peak of honor and beauty and that our people can still sustain certain simple philosophies at which some miserable souls feel it incumbent to sneer. I refer to some of the Psalms, and to the Gettysburg Address and to the Scout Oath. I refer to the Lord's Prayer and to that other oath which a man must take when he stands with hand uplifted and swears that he will defend his Country.*

Even well after the trip, Wayne continued to correspond with GIs. In late 1967, for instance, Sergeant Gilbert Mumford sent a long handwritten letter from the Vietnamese jungle thanking him for "lifting the morale and spirit" of his unit when they met him—a unit nicknamed the Apache Raiders.

"Dear Sergeant," Wayne wrote back in January 1968, "Congratulations on your platoon. I don't think the Apache Raiders need any word from me to lift their spirits and morale. But tell them that the letter from you fellows raised mine."

Following the Vietnam tour, Wayne had Mary St. John send hundreds of Christmas boxes to troops in various units in 1967—fresh preserves from Knott's Berry Farm—and the archives include several letters thanking him for the tasty treat. He also visited the US Army Hospital at Camp Kue in Hawaii in April 1967.

TOP, FROM LEFT TO RIGHT: *The pilot cap Wayne wore in* The High and the Mighty; *an Army cap from his cameo in* Cast a Giant Shadow; *and a field cap from* The Green Berets. OPPOSITE, TOP: *Relaxing on his boat, John Wayne wears the brass bracelet given to him by members of the Montagnard Strike Force on his right wrist.* OPPOSITE, INSET: *The Presidential Medal of Freedom presented posthumously to John Wayne by President Jimmy Carter shortly after Wayne's death in 1980.*

A few years after his trip, in 1970, Wayne started wearing another bracelet—this time a POW bracelet sent to him by Carole Hanson in remembrance of her husband, Captain Stephen P. Hanson, whose plane had been shot down over Laos. Mrs. Hanson cherished a picture her husband had sent her from Vietnam with the hand-scrawled caption, "me as John Wayne," and she thought the movie star might want to become involved in the POW movement.

Over the years, as Mrs. Hanson went on to become deeply involved in the POW/MIA cause, she stayed in touch with John Wayne. For instance, she wrote him on February 1, 1971, to inform Wayne that her then four-year-old son, Todd, "talks continually about how you are helping to bring his daddy home," and asking Wayne to sign a picture for little Todd. For years after that, Wayne periodically corresponded with Todd, who never got to meet his father. Mrs. Hanson also had Wayne invited to a POW/MIA luncheon event in Newport Beach in 1971. When he could not attend due to a previous commitment, he wrote her to express his "heartfelt sympathies and enthusiastic support to all in your efforts. Mrs. Hanson, I faithfully wear the steel wristband with your husband's identification." As it turned out, it was eventually determined that Captain Hanson was killed when his plane was shot down, and his remains were repatriated in 2000. Today, his name is among thousands of others on the Vietnam Memorial.

Wayne eventually became inundated with letters from families and friends of other POWs, as well as letters from families of soldiers killed in action or missing. As the 1968 letter that begins this chapter illustrates, he would frequently and eloquently write them back expressing his solidarity with their plight.

Following his personal experience in Vietnam, it's clear that Wayne's feelings about the war grew even more passionate. He was vociferous in his arguments, but whether one agrees with them or not, it's clear they were deeply personal. He felt, it appears from his letters and the media coverage of his Vietnam trip, that he personally knew the people he was praising and supporting.

One newspaper article about his visit to Vietnam, published in July 1966, headlined that the visit had moved Wayne to "rare eloquence" and another quoted him as declaring that American troops in the field were "on the ball." The accounts also quoted him as explaining his role in visiting the troops this way—"I cannot sing or dance, but I certainly can talk to the kids." He added that he hoped the time he spent with wounded soldiers would give them "something to write about besides the war."

In such articles, Wayne strongly urged support for the war effort and declared, as he did in many letters to friends and fans alike, that "we're at war with Communism." He reiterated this view not only in public statements but also in private correspondence with ordinary citizens who chose to write him to discuss the issue.

On June 30, 1966, in a two-page reply to a letter sent by Mrs. Willa J. Armour, Wayne rejected the notion the United States was meddling in a civil war: "The Vietnamese cannot be expected to take one quick vow and establish a way of life. We are responsible to see that their lives and our sons will not have died in vain. We must have the courage not to forsake them, having gone this far."

To Brenda Norman, on October 10, 1968, he disputed the assertion that his 1966 trip to Vietnam promoted propaganda about the war. He declared, very clearly, that he fully believed what he was saying, based on what he saw with his own eyes, and he suggested that his outspoken words in recent years about the conflict were designed to "give the thinking people of the United States a greater outlook on the present danger of Communism."

Further, in his aforementioned July 1969 letter to Major Eugene McNerney, Wayne aggressively pushed back on the "hawk" label, a term he found simplistic and out of context.

"Getting shot at doesn't have anything to do with being a prominent hawk," he stated in the letter. "I believe it is honorable to stand by our commitments and to try to help an oppressed and tortured people, and to protect our country from a system that has vowed they will destroy us." ✪

Here is a list of the eighteen movies John Wayne appeared in that depict him as a fighting American military volunteer, uniformed soldier, or officer in a major conflict. This list includes some of the Westerns listed on page 52, in which he plays an American cavalry officer or volunteer. He did play small or ancillary roles as military figures over the years in other films not listed here. In a couple, such as *The Oregon Trail* (1936) and *The Lonely Trail* (1936), Wayne played characters affiliated with the military, but those stories were not directly related to participation in a military conflict. In *The Sea Chase* (1955), the outbreak of World War II is the backdrop, but Wayne's character is a German sea

captain, not a fighting man. He also played, of course, Ghengis Khan leading conquering armies in *The Conqueror* (1956). In *The Wings of Eagles* (1957), he played a paralyzed former navy flyer who looks back on his wartime experiences. In *The Longest Day* (1962), he had only a cameo in a larger story about the invasion of Normandy; in *How the West Was Won* (1962), he had a brief role as General William Tecumseh Sherman in a Western epic; and in *Cast a Giant Shadow* (1966), he played a small role as an American general in a film about Israel's War of Independence. But in the eighteen films listed here, Wayne played an active American fighting man.

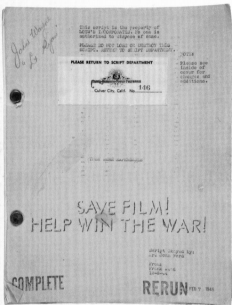

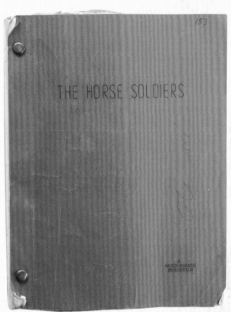

Allegheny Uprising (1939)
(volunteer, pre-Revolutionary War period)

Flying Tigers (1942) (World War II aerial combat volunteer)

The Fighting Seabees (1944)
(US Navy Seabee)

They Were Expendable (1945)
(naval PT boat officer)

Back to Bataan (1945) (army colonel)

Fort Apache (1948) (cavalry officer)

The Fighting Kentuckian (1949)
(nineteenth-century militiaman)

She Wore a Yellow Ribbon (1949)
(cavalry officer)

Sands of Iwo Jima (1949) (marine sergeant)

Rio Grande (1950) (cavalry officer)

Operation Pacific (1951)
(naval submarine officer)

Flying Leathernecks (1951)
(US Marine Corps. flying squadron officer)

Jet Pilot (1957) (US Air Force colonel)

The Horse Soldiers (1959)
(Civil War cavalry officer)

The Alamo (1960)
(volunteer in Texas-Mexico War)

In Harm's Way (1965) (career naval officer)

The Green Berets (1968)
(Special Forces officer)

The Undefeated (1969) (cavalry officer)

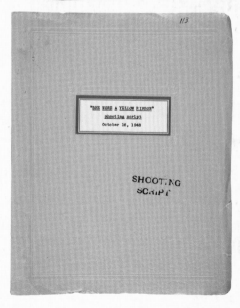

ABOVE: *John Wayne's personal scripts from* They Were Expendable, The Horse Soldiers, Flying Leathernecks, *and* She Wore a Yellow Ribbon. OPPOSITE: *Script from* The Wings of Eagles *(center right). Movie posters from* Flying Tigers *and* Jet Pilot, *and characteristic photos of Wayne from his war-related pictures—*The Longest Day *(top right),* In Harm's Way *(center), and* Allegheny Uprising *(bottom left).*

CHAPTER SIX

MAN

OF

NATIONAL

INTEREST

"THIS IS A GOOD COUNTRY. WITH GOOD PEOPLE IN IT.
GOOD PEOPLE DON'T ALWAYS AGREE WITH ONE ANOTHER.
MAYBE THE BEST THING WE DO IN THIS COUNTRY IS AGREE TO
DISAGREE ONCE IN A WHILE. BUT WITH A CERTAIN AMOUNT OF
CIVILITY. AND THAT'S WHAT SEEMS TO BE MISSING THESE DAYS....
A CERTAIN AMOUNT OF CIVILITY. WE'RE SHOUTING WHEN WE SHOULD
BE TALKING. WE'RE ARGUING WHEN WE SHOULD BE CONVERSING.
WE'RE ANGRY WHEN WE SHOULD BE REASONING. I THINK THE BEST
SINGLE THING ALL OF US CAN DO IS CALM DOWN. AND MAYBE
THINK A LITTLE BIT MORE AND TALK A LITTLE BIT LESS."

—JOHN WAYNE, NATIONAL FOOTBALL FOUNDATION AND
COLLEGE HALL OF FAME SPEECH, DECEMBER 4, 1974

W HEN JOHN WAYNE SHOWED UP TO ACCEPT THE GOLD MEDAL AWARD, given to "an outstanding American who has contributed significantly to the sport of college football and our country" by the National Football Foundation and College Hall of Fame on December 4, 1974, he was ostensibly there to discuss his gridiron adventures.

As important as football was to his life experience, Wayne was most interested in the "and our country" aspect of the award that night. The country was in the middle of the Watergate turmoil—a difficult issue for Wayne, as he had a relationship with Richard Nixon. Political rhetoric was at a boiling point, and Wayne had lately been in the thick of it, especially after his famously controversial interview with *Playboy* magazine in 1971, which had ruffled more than a few feathers.

Yet, at the awards dinner in 1974, Wayne was largely in a reflective and conciliatory mood. He pleaded for mutual respect between opposing sides then engaged in a vicious national debate.

Such an appeal was remarkable coming from Wayne considering his well-earned reputation as a rock-ribbed member of the conservative establishment and unabashed supporter of conservative causes over the decades. From Eisenhower onward, Wayne campaigned for Republican candidates, befriended Republican presidents and senators, corresponded with conservative icons like

pundit William F. Buckley, spoke out in defense of traditionally conservative causes—such as gun rights, anticommunism, escalating the Vietnam War, and much more—and periodically railed against the "liberal media" and liberal philosophies generally.

However, Wayne's plea at the awards dinner for civility was also a hallmark of his belief system, even if that aspect rarely earned him headlines. Certainly, his National Football Foundation speech resonates today. It shows the dichotomy of his personality—consistently conservative philosophically but maintaining deep personal relationships across the political spectrum. It also shows how he mellowed somewhat late in life and was plainly interested above all else in his country's welfare.

"Respect for the other fellow is what democracy is all about," Wayne told dinner guests. "And I think respect for country goes hand-in-hand."

Perhaps that is why, even as he grew to be an icon of the conservative movement, Wayne also formed deep bonds with many who didn't share his politics. A host of Hollywood's liberals from the era, like Kirk Douglas, were among his friends and respected acquaintances. His son Patrick says that is certainly true of his relationship with his dearest friend of all, John Ford.

"John Ford and my dad were opposed diametrically on just about every political point of view," Patrick says. "John Ford was a military hero, but voted liberal most of the time. They were very different in that respect. And yet, they had one of the great friendships of all time."

Wayne's letters suggest what he enjoyed most about political matters was the spirit of the debate, and he usually avoided personalizing politics. In late 1961, for example, his friend and fellow movie star Paul Newman sent Wayne books on liberal social policy. Wayne wrote back to thank him for the books and sent Newman a few books of his own. Then, over the course of a three-page missive, he outlined his views in great detail for Newman. Among other things, Wayne argued for the notion of "balance" in policy matters. "To provide welfare for the unfortunate is part of [our] duty and responsibility," he wrote to Newman. "To make sure that balance is kept is also our responsibility. In order that we do not become a public welfare socialistic bureaucracy, we must keep this balance. We must maintain a middle class."

In that same letter, Wayne expressed fears that some of President Kennedy's advisors might be socialists. And yet, ten years later, during one of his conversations with journalist Wayne Warga, Wayne praised Kennedy and expressed ongoing dismay at the president's assassination.

Warga quoted Wayne saying, "You didn't have to be a Kennedy fan to be decimated by his assassination. John Kennedy could have been so very good—he was just beginning to realize his responsibilities. Potentially, he was a leader. We never had the chance to find out though."

Wayne also disputed the notion that he was some kind of extremist. While talking with Warga, he claimed that ultra-right

icon George Wallace had approached him in the 1960s about possibly being his running mate, and he wasn't even remotely interested. "I cannot figure out why it is [Wallace] felt I believed as he did," Wayne told Warga. "I don't. Hell, I never have."

Indeed, it's instructive to note that Wayne's surviving liberal friends hold him in high esteem to this day. Famed cinematographer Haskell Wexler, for instance, now in his nineties, has been one of Hollywood's most vocal liberals for decades and was a fierce opponent of the Vietnam War. Wexler was also good friends with John Wayne. They became friendly when Wexler directed a series of Great Western Bank commercials starring Wayne in the 1970s, and they had several dinners late in Wayne's life that Wexler still finds illuminating. At one such dinner in 1977, Wayne gave Wexler a book of poetry, and Wexler wrote him back saying, "You have love from all of us who worked with you."

Today, Wexler doesn't consider it contrary to love someone who disagreed with him so fundamentally on so many things. Wexler insists that John Wayne was "democratically minded, with a small 'd.' He had a pretty interesting sense of fairness. When we had open discussions, there were, of course, superficial points of disagreement. But on his sense of fairness and humaneness, we went beyond things that you normally think of as political. They make caricatures out of people like him, and that makes for good headlines. But, in my opinion, he was much like another friend of mine, Henry Fonda. They were both good Americans, and that's a better label to put on him than 'conservative.'"

Wexler points to the public stand Wayne took in the late 1970s to support President Jimmy Carter's decision to push for ratification of the contentious Panama Canal agreement.

PAGE 94: *John Wayne speaks at the Buffalo Bill Historical Center in Cody, Wyoming, on July 4, 1976.* OPPOSITE: *John Wayne was a close friend and supporter of Ronald Reagan and his wife, Nancy, as this photograph, signed by the Reagans, indicates.* INSET: *Three of John Wayne's Republican Party membership cards, from 1966, 1973, and 1976, respectively. Wayne was a longtime Republican and supporter of causes on both sides of the fence.*

WAYNE FOR PRESIDENT

In early 1963, a couple of enterprising college students from Texas wrote John Wayne in an effort to get him to consider pursuing the Republican nomination for president in 1964. David Schofield and Robert Yates, two students at the University of Dallas, were behind the idea, and they promoted their drive to "draft Wayne" to local newspapers and wire services. They made posters and bumper stickers, wrote college newspaper editorials, and even started a petition drive to lure Wayne into running, using the slogan, "We need a president who can act."

John Wayne was vacationing on the *Wild Goose* when the whole thing started, and so his secretary, Mary St. John, spoke to the media on his behalf. She said she thought it sounded like "a wonderful idea" and that her boss would find it "tremendously flattering."

But Wayne threw cold water on the idea in a good-natured way with a telegram to David Schofield on April 3, 1964.

"Thanks very much for your complimentary opinion of me, particularly the line 'man who can act,'" he wrote. "I thank you for your efforts, but no, thank you, no. As the saying goes, I'd rather be right than president."

Notes replying to college student David Schofield reference attempts of Schofield and other students to get John Wayne to run for president in the 1960s, and wire service and newspaper coverage of their efforts. Basically, Schofield made the request, and with humor, Wayne turned him down.

John Wayne Sets Campaign Speech in Texas

United Press International
SAN ANTONO, March 18. — Movie star John Wayne, who is being promoted as a Republican presidential candidate in Texas by a group of college students, will make a campaign speech here next month — for another candidate.

Wayne will be featured speaker at a fund-raising dinner April 6 for Gordon McLendon, Dallas radio and television executive seeking the Democratic nomination for the U.S. Senate.

A student committee at the University of Dallas opened a campaign several weeks ago to secure the GOP presidental nomination for Wayne, under the slogan "we need a president who can act."

1/3/67

Dear Mr. Schofield:

Mr. Wayne is out of the country at the moment, but in checking our files, this is the only communication that came from our office.

Mary St. John, Secretary

NIGHT LETTER
April 3, 1964

Western Union Oper.
E. F.

DAVID SCHOFIELD
P. O. Box 265
University of Dallas Station
Texas

THANKS VERY MUCH FOR YOUR COMPLIMENTARY OPINION OF ME, PARTICULARLY THE LINE "MAN WHO CAN ACT". I THANK YOU FOR YOUR EFFORTS, BUT NO, THANK YOU, no". AS THE SAYING GOES, I'D RATHER BE RIGHT THAN PRESIDENT.

Sincerely,

John Wayne

UPI-41
(CANDIDATE)
SAN ANTONIO, TEX.--MOVIE STAR JOHN WAYNE, WHO IS BEING PROMOTED AS A REPUBLICAN PRESIDENT CANDIDATE IN TEXAS BY A GROUP OF COLLEGE STUDENTS, WILL MAKE A CAMPAIGN SPEECH HERE APRIL 6 AT A FUND-RAISING DINNER FOR GORDON MCLENDON, DALLAS RADIO AND TELEVISION EXECUTIVE SEEKING THE DEMOCRATIC NOMINATION FOR THE U.S. SENATE.
3/18--TD1040AEX

Though hardly the only instance, it was certainly the highest profile example of Wayne intentionally inserting himself into national affairs over something he passionately believed in. He did it even as his health was declining, and in this case, he wasn't lobbying for the conservative point of view. Indeed, many leading conservatives of the day were angered by Wayne's public stand.

Wayne wrote editorials on the subject, testified before Congress in 1977 about the treaty, corresponded furiously with friends like William F. Buckley about the issue, and wrote to prominent conservatives in the Senate urging them to support ratification. Some accused Wayne of adopting his position simply because of his connections to Panamanian leader Omar Torrijos. In fact, Wayne did have a personal interest in Panama dating back to the 1940s, which he freely admitted in his congressional testimony in 1977. However, he also spent months researching the topic, and he sent friends detailed position papers and rebuttal statements on every aspect of the debate.

Wayne even wrote President Carter on October 12, 1977, pledging his support for ratification. He signed the letter from "Loyal Opposition," in homage to a congratulatory note Wayne

sent Carter immediately after he defeated President Ford, whom Wayne had supported, in the November 1976 presidential election.

Carter appreciated Wayne's congratulations when he was elected, and wrote him back on November 10, 1976, expressing appreciation for the note. "I trust the only area in which we

TOP, LEFT TO RIGHT: *John Wayne, Nancy Reagan, actress Gina Lollobrigida, and Ronald Reagan enjoy some cocktail party banter.* BOTTOM RIGHT: *The Waynes and the Reagans dine at a political event.*

will find ourselves in opposition is that of Party loyalty," Carter wrote. "I will need your help in the coming years, and hope to have your support."

Carter's people asked Wayne to participate in a gala as part of Carter's inaugural festivities in January 1977, and Wayne readily agreed. The two men corresponded periodically in the early days of the Carter presidency—usually with Wayne criticizing Carter's policies and Carter thanking him for his insight.

By the time Wayne jumped in to support him on the Panama Canal issue, they had developed a mutual respect. Indeed, when Wayne fell ill in 1979, Carter called his office about two months before his passing and spoke directly with his son Michael Wayne in an effort to learn about his condition. A handwritten note from Wayne's then secretary, Pat Stacy, on April 4, 1979, detailed Carter's call. Her notes say the president "expressed concern over JW condition on behalf of himself and the American people. He said JW was a great national asset. He said, anything he could do, to let him know. He said JW surprises us all with his ability to recover, and lastly that JW is in his thoughts and prayers." Then, weeks later, Carter detoured from a campaign stop to visit John Wayne at the UCLA Medical Center for what would be Carter's final visit with the actor. However, as the foreword to this book demonstrates, President Jimmy Carter's affection and respect for John Wayne endures.

During the Panama Canal debate, while fielding accusations that he was trying to help Torrijos, John Wayne was, in actuality, putting an even closer relationship on the line with his position—his friendship with Ronald Reagan. Their relationship went back

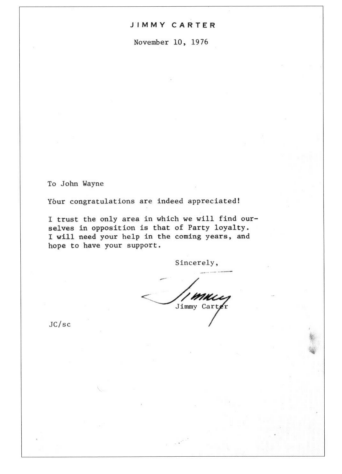

JIMMY CARTER

November 10, 1976

To John Wayne

Your congratulations are indeed appreciated!

I trust the only area in which we will find ourselves in opposition is that of Party loyalty. I will need your help in the coming years, and hope to have your support.

Sincerely,

Jimmy Carter

JC/sc

to Reagan's Hollywood days, and Wayne was a solid supporter through Reagan's gubernatorial campaigns in California and his first run for president in 1976.

Reagan was readying for another presidential run in 1980, and he had published a paper declaring the Panama Canal handover to be against the nation's best interests; as such, Reagan became a high-profile opponent of ratification. The correspondence between the two men during this period became, at times, heated over the subject. Things got particularly testy in October and November of 1977. Reagan sent Wayne some material on October 3, 1977, defending his position on the treaty and suggesting that Wayne's position was due simply to "your deep loyalty to friends. Hence, I understand your dilemma with regard to General Torrijos. I know this is not an easy time for you."

The next day, Wayne responded by sending the reams of research he had done on the topic. He ended the letter stating, "I shall bother you with this subject no more," but that promise wasn't to last even a few days. Wayne sent a second letter on October 7, 1977, after reading Reagan's proposal for a coalition of Western Hemisphere nations to operate the canal. He declared that while "I haven't been trying to bug you on the Panama Canal thing, I have been trying to give you another point of view."

Wayne went on to review his relationship with Reagan dating back to their days together in the Screen Actors Guild (SAG). He then stated how disappointed he was that Reagan would not meet with two Panamanian negotiators, as Wayne had requested.

"After the record above of what I have done for you, I really am embarrassed that you would give [the negotiators] the brush," he stated in concluding the four-page letter. "This is a long letter Ronnie, and I feel that I have to get it off my chest."

INSET: *In a November 1976 letter, president-elect Jimmy Carter wrote John Wayne thanking him for his letter of congratulations upon Carter's election victory (see page 8).*

THE WHITE HOUSE

WASHINGTON

October 22, 1956.

Dear Mr. Wayne:

My visit to Los Angeles would not have been
so happy an occasion without your joining us
at the Hollywood Bowl Friday night.   Incidentally, if I had people like you talking for
me, I would not have to make a single political
speech myself.   And I assure you that I would
like!

With my gratitude and best wishes,

Sincerely,

Dwight Eisenhower

Mr. John Wayne,
Hollywood,
California.

THE WHITE HOUSE

WASHINGTON

November 12, 1964

Dear John:

I am grateful to you for your thoughtful
telegram.

Even during the campaign I never lost my
zest for John Wayne movies. You and I
have been in our respective fields -- movies
and public service -- for about the same time.
I can only hope that neither of us tries to
swap professions.

You are a good American and I am cheered
by your wire.

Sincerely,

Lyndon B. Johnson

Mr. John Wayne
Encino, California

Federal Bureau of Investigation
United States Department of Justice
Washington, D. C.

April 8, 1970

PERSONAL

Mr. John Wayne
c/o Paramount Pictures Corporation
5451 Marathon Street
Los Angeles, California 90038

Dear Mr. Wayne:

Heartiest congratulations on your winning

an "Oscar" as best actor of 1969. This is indeed a well-

deserved and splendid tribute to you and your ability, and

you have my very best wishes for continued success.

Sincerely yours,

J. Edgar Hoover

Dear Duke   May 15

We know you've been getting stacks & stacks of mail. We didn't know of a sure way that an extra letter might reach you. But as you can see we found a way. Don't trip the messenger he was happy to do it.

Not a day (or very many hours of each day) goes by that you are not upper most in our thoughts. We can handle the gasoline shortage, the anti-nuclear freaks & even the crazy way the admin. is dealing with the Russians— we can't take much more of you being out of action. How are we going to head off that gang of candidates at Eagle Gap (New Hampshire) without you riding point?

Duke you are not only in our thoughts — you are in our prayers every day. And those prayers are born of our love & affection for you.

Sincerely

Nancy + Ron

LA CASA PACIFICA
SAN CLEMENTE, CALIFORNIA

December 15, 1976

Dear John -

Pat and I were terribly distressed to hear that you were in the hospital. We hope and pray you will soon be "back in the saddle".

As Paul Keyes probably told you I thought your T. V. tribute was superb. For 50 years you have been a super star and will continue to be in the future

God bless you - Sincerely RN

GERALD R. FORD

October 14, 1977

Dear Duke:

Man! What a relief to hear the hoofbeats
of the big white horse and see a friendly
gun gallop into view.

It was getting pretty lonely out there....
Thanks, Pard!

Warmest personal regards,

Sincerely,

Jerry Ford

Mr. John Wayne
2686 Bayshore Drive
Newport Beach, California 92260

EDWARD M. KENNEDY
MASSACHUSETTS

United States Senate

WASHINGTON, D.C. 20510

October 28, 1977

Mr. John Wayne
9570 Wilshire Boulevard-Suite 400
Beverly Hills, California 90212

Dear Mr. Wayne:

Thank you for your views on the Panama Canal Treaties.

Historically, no one disputes that the Canal stands as a monument to American determination and skill -- but also that we virtually imposed our control of the Canal Zone over Colombia and Panama in 1903. Today, no one disputes that the Canal continues to play a significant role in American commerce and defense -- but that this role is far less than it was in the past.

A key question is how this role can be best protected over the decades ahead. One approach is to insist on the status quo of the past 75 years -- which resulted in the 1964 riots against what Panamanians have viewed as colonialist occupation of their territory, cutting their nation into two parts. I am convinced that this approach would bring continued confrontation with Panama -- and inevitably with most of Latin America.

The other approach is to end our unequal relationship with Panama and to obtain its full cooperation in the efficient and impartial operation of the Canal. That is the approach of the Treaties, which guarantee our unlimited access and use of the Canal as well as the legitimate interests of our citizens and our property in the area. To our Latin American friends, as well as to the rest of the world, this approach demonstrates that we are prepared to work in fair and equal partnership with less powerful nations.

The Secretary of Defense and the Joint Chiefs of Staff, who participated actively in the negotiations, have unanimously endorsed their results as being in our best national security interest. Indeed, the judgment of former Secretaries of State Dean Rusk and Henry Kissinger is that these Treaties are, if anything, more advantageous to us than the ones they replaced. In addition, since 1964, four Presidents have been pledged to transfer the Canal to Panama. The Treaties frankly carry out this commitment by the year 2000 -- making Panama whole after a century of division. It would be against our country's best traditions not only to refuse to act in our national interest, but to break the word of four Presidents.

Again, I appreciated having your views.

Sincerely,

Edward M. Kennedy

5-15-78

To John Wayne

One of my deepest commitments is to fight terrorism, and my oath of office requires me to uphold the laws of the United States. I do not find the two to be incompatible.

Jimmy

p.s. We're proud of your quick recovery. J

A few weeks before John Wayne passed away, his old friend Senator Barry Goldwater of Arizona introduced a bill to Congress authorizing President Carter to present Wayne with a specially struck Congressional Gold Medal. The gold medal is a rare honor occasionally bestowed by Congress on a civilian who has had a major impact on American history or culture, and it is always physically designed to honor the achievements of the specific honoree. Goldwater and a slew of dignitaries spoke to Congress on May 21, 1979, in favor of the idea, ranging from Elizabeth Taylor to war hero General Albert Coady Wedemeyer, and many others. Telegrams were read into the congressional record from Frank Sinatra, Katharine Hepburn, Gregory Peck, James Arness, Kirk Douglas, and more. But no one touched the core of why John Wayne was, in fact, a man of such significant national interest as to deserve such an honor as his old friend and costar actress Maureen O'Hara.

O'Hara starred with Wayne in five movies and, over the years, became one of his dearest friends. She flew across the world from the Virgin Islands and barely made it in time to address a subcommittee hearing in the House of Representatives. She spoke from the heart, without prepared remarks, about her old friend John Wayne.

"To the people of the world, John Wayne is not just an actor and a very fine actor," she told the subcommittee. "John Wayne is the United States of America. He is what they believe it to be. He is what they hope it will be. And he is what they hope it will always be. It is every person's dream that the United States will be like John Wayne and always like him."

Eventually, she told the subcommittee exactly what the gold medal should say: "John Wayne, American."

Congress, of course, approved the bill, President Carter signed it, and the United States Mint struck the gold coin days before Wayne took his final breath. The medal was presented to his family in a ceremony on March 6, 1980. One side shows a picture of Wayne with the words O'Hara recommended, "John Wayne, American." The other side shows him on horseback, riding through his beloved Monument Valley.

ABOVE: *Elizabeth Taylor (left) and Maureen O'Hara (right) were among those who provided moving testimony in support of Wayne receiving his Congressional medal.*
RIGHT: *Wayne's Congressional Gold Medal, awarded shortly before his death. The words "John Wayne, American" were suggested by O'Hara. The reverse side shows Wayne riding a horse through Monument Valley.*

Wayne wrote Reagan again on November 11, 1977, when he received a missive from Reagan's political committee, which was fund raising based on Reagan's opposition to the treaty. He was rather harsh, saying Reagan had "lost a great and unique 'appointment with history,'" had failed to give adequate "time and thought on this issue," and was taking a position that would eventually lead the public to conclude, "you are merely making statements for political expediency." He finished by saying he didn't want to make it "personal" and that, "you know damned well I have great affection for you and Nancy."

The emotion of the letter got Reagan concerned about their friendship, and on November 21, he wrote back. Reagan stated immediately that, "I'm glad you closed with a declaration of your continuing friendship for Nancy and myself. I'm sure you must know the deep affection we have for you and our disagreement over these treaties will not affect or lessen that affection." At the end of his three-page letter, Reagan added his fervent

hope that they could prevent "being on opposite sides" from "affecting a friendship that Nancy and I treasure."

In the end, the Panama Canal treaty was ratified with Wayne's help. That battle was of course an exception for John Wayne—most of the time, publicly, he was solidly in harmony with traditional conservative positions on most issues.

Among the topics he was particularly vocal on was the right to bear arms, as a lifelong firearms owner and member of the National Rifle Association (NRA). In May 1965, the publisher of the magazine *Guns & Ammo*, Thomas J. Siatos, wrote him to warn about a proposed bill sponsored by Senator Thomas Dodd of Connecticut that would strengthen gun laws by restricting the purchase of mail-order guns. Siatos laid out his position, which Wayne agreed with, and so he promptly flipped over the letter and on the back began handwriting a first draft of a detailed letter he was to shortly send Senator Dodd in opposition to the bill.

"Felonious acts with a car by some does not call for the right to confiscate the automobiles of all of us," he wrote to Dodd. "Felonious acts by some with knives should not force all of us to eat with only a spoon.... I respectfully request and urge that

John Wayne periodically used his status as an international star to promote widely held values that resonated with the public. In May 1967, for example, Wayne was invited to be a guest on *The Dean Martin Show*. Both men came on stage on horses and chatted for a while, and then Martin congratulated Wayne on the recent birth of his youngest daughter, Marisa, who was then eight months old. He asked him what he wanted for her future.

John Wayne gave a short but poignant reply. "I'd like her to know some of the values we knew as kids," he said. "Some of those values too many people think are old fashioned today.... Most of all, I want her to be grateful—as I am every day of my life—to live in these United States."

Wayne went on for a few more minutes and got a thunderous ovation. After the appearance, he was inundated with hundreds of letters from fans thanking him and asking for transcripts.

Then, in 1973, he recorded the spoken-word album *America: Why I Love Her*, reciting patriotic poetry penned by actor/writer John Mitchum (brother of actor Robert Mitchum). The album sold well and was nominated for a Grammy Award. It was reissued shortly after Wayne's death in 1979 and again following the September 11, 2001, terrorist attacks as a compact disc. Among the Wayne archival materials is a draft of his personal comments for a related book that came out a few years after the album (see page 48 for more on the project). Over the course of that manuscript, Wayne rejoices in the diversity of America.

"Where else in the world can you get a good hamburger sandwich, a cheese blintz, a taco or some real lasagna all on the same block?" he wrote. "Where else in the world can you get Chopin Etudes, Dixieland Jazz, or Country Western music just by twisting your radio dials?

"When we all tear down the walls of bigotry and prejudice and live in real harmony with ourselves and others, then we'll all say, 'I am an American.' Pure and simple."

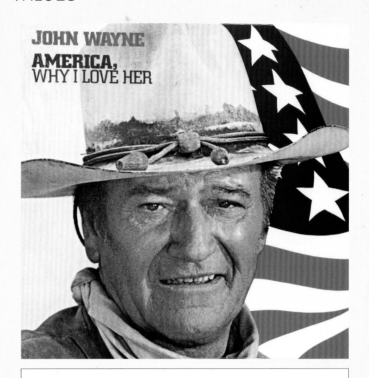

TOP RIGHT: *Cover of the famed* America: Why I Love Her *record album that Wayne made in 1973, reciting patriotic poetry.* BOTTOM RIGHT: *An excerpt of the* Dean Martin Show *script from the 1967 episode in which John Wayne talked about his values. Fans often requested transcripts of his short speech.*

77.

<u>DEAN/DUKE TALK</u>
#07 A07

DEAN (CONT'D)

Here you are one of the biggest
stars in the whole world, - been making
pictures for 37 years... got a spanking
new daughter... what do you want for her,
Duke?

DUKE

Same as any parent wants, I guess.
I'd just like to stick around long
enough to get her started. I'd like her
to know some of the values we knew as kids.
Some of those values too many people think
are old fashioned today.
Most of all I want her to be grateful -
as I am every day of my life - to live in
these United States. I know it may sound
corny, but the first thing my daughter's
learning from me is the Lord's Prayer,
some of the Psalms, and I don't care if
she never <u>memorizes</u> the Gettysburg Address,
just so long as she <u>understands</u> it. And
since little girls are seldom called on to
defend their country, she may never have
to raise her hand for that oath, but I
certainly want her to respect all who do.
I guess that's what I want for my daughter, Dean.

DEAN

I'm proud to know you, Duke.

(INTO: DEAN/DUKE TALK)

The national power of John Wayne's voice was illustrated on December 1, 1978, when he sent a short note to TV personality Barbara Walters expressing his opinion about the Patty Hearst case. The note read:

Dear Barbara:

It seems quite odd to me that no editors or television opinion makers have pointed out the fact that the American people have immediately accepted the idea that one man can brainwash 400 human beings into committing mass suicide [referencing the 1978 Jonestown Massacre], but will not accept the fact that a ruthless group, the Symbionese Liberation Army, could brainwash one little girl by torture and degradation and confinement.

—*John Wayne*

Hearst, at the time, was serving jail time for her role in bank robberies she allegedly participated in while a captive of a radical group. The movement to get her released from prison was heating up, and Wayne simply wanted to let Walters know his opinion that she should be freed. Once the note became public, Wayne was flooded with letters from the public praising him for sticking up for Hearst, who was finally released a few months later.

The Committee for the Release of Patricia Hearst and the Hearst family all wrote to offer thanks, and Wayne was invited to Hearst's 1979 wedding shortly after her prison release, but by then, he was much too ill to attend and in fact died a few weeks later.

John Wayne gives television personality Barbara Walters a tour of his boat, Wild Goose. *He wrote her in 1978 to express support for the release of Patty Hearst from jail, as the newspaper clipping (above) explained at the time.*

"RESPECT FOR THE OTHER FELLOW IS WHAT DEMOCRACY IS ALL ABOUT. AND I THINK RESPECT FOR COUNTRY GOES HAND-IN-HAND."

your committee review this bill and strike out that part of it which endangers an inalienable right of any American—the right to own and use firearms."

Reams of correspondence in the John Wayne archives detail his active work to support and help prominent Republicans dating all the way back to the election of Dwight Eisenhower, for whom he made radio commercials, gave speeches, and participated in his second inauguration in 1957. In 1964, he was an unwavering supporter of his friend Barry Goldwater. But of all the politicians that Wayne formed relationships with, Richard Nixon was the president he corresponded most frequently with. The two began corresponding when Nixon was Eisenhower's vice president in the 1950s. In fact, Nixon wrote Wayne on January 19, 1961, as his term as vice president was expiring, to thank him for his support.

"I realize how much easier it would be for someone in your position to avoid taking sides on controversial questions which might adversely affect the popularity which is so essential for continued success in your chosen profession," Nixon wrote him.

By the time Nixon became president, Wayne was regularly writing him letters, offering his familiar "point of view." Sometimes, he wrote just to kibitz with the chief executive. In the summer of 1972, for instance, he mailed the president a copy of a telegram he had received from someone claiming to represent something called "The American Party," promoting the notion that Wayne run for president, which was not the first time the idea had come up (see page 98).

Wayne forwarded the telegram to Nixon along with a short note on August 1, 1972, stating, "Dear Mr. President: Look out! Watch your P's and Q's!" Nixon responded two days later with a short note of his own. "Dear Duke," the president wrote, "Don't do it. After all, Duke is a better title than President!"

TOP: *John Wayne greets Richard Nixon during the 1972 presidential campaign.*

THE VICE PRESIDENT
OF THE
UNITED STATES OF AMERICA

January 19, 1961

Dear John:

As my term of office as Vice President draws to a close, I want to take this opportunity to tell you how much I appreciated all that you did in my behalf during the 1960 Presidential campaign.

I realize how much easier it would be for someone in your position to avoid taking sides on controversial questions which might adversely affect the popularity which is so essential for continued success in your chosen profession. For that reason, I am particularly grateful for the support which you gave so courageously and unselfishly. I only regret that my efforts could not have been just that extra bit more effective which would have brought victory for those who worked so hard for our cause.

I hope it will not be too long before we meet again so that I can express my appreciation personally. In the meantime, Pat joins me in sending our best wishes for the New Year.

Sincerely,

Dick Nixon

Mr. John Wayne
1022 Palm Avenue
Los Angeles, California

Wayne also spoke on Nixon's behalf at the Republican National Convention in 1972, introducing a film about the president and declaring he was the kind of leader "who won't pussyfoot around."

Later, as the Watergate scandal enveloped Nixon, Wayne continued to write him, often inserting encouragement into his notes. In December 1973, for instance, he sent Nixon a Mailgram suggesting he look into new energy technologies that Wayne had heard about. But he also wrote, "Don't give up the ship. Over the past few weeks you have shown the greatest moral courage of any human being I know. How lonely it must be up there, but remember [I am] one of the many millions of Americans that have confidence in you."

Nixon wrote back the next day, stating firmly, "as for those rumors, don't you believe them. The next time you hear one, just say that you have it on the best authority that the president intends to stay and do the job he was elected to do."

Eight months later, Nixon resigned. Even then, Wayne's fondness for him never waned. In late 1974, for instance, he dashed off a telegram to new President Gerald Ford, praising his decision to give Nixon a controversial executive pardon.

"Congratulations and many thanks for your respect and feelings for the human dignity of Mr. Nixon," the telegram read. "It's a lonely road. Here's one you can count on. John Wayne."

Still, Wayne seemed to clearly feel a personal disappointment over the Watergate scandal, and perhaps its result mellowed him somewhat. By December 1974 at the aforementioned National Football Foundation and Hall of Fame Gold Medal Award dinner at the Waldorf Hotel in New York, he was certainly promoting a more optimistic philosophy about public discourse. In typical Wayne fashion, in fact, he declared that, in the end, everything would be okay.

"Take a good look at this Watergate mess," he told the audience. "It was wrong. Positively, absolutely, dead wrong. Some men abused power. But the system works. Other men abused money, but the system works. Others lied and perjured themselves, but the system works. I'm not here to defend politics, which is what Watergate is all about. I don't know all the details about that yet, nor do you. [A football team] survives a fumble just as a government survives politics and Watergate.

"You know what I say? To hell with politics. Isn't it about time we used our present to get out of our past and into our future?" ✪

OPPOSITE: *Wayne's correspondence with Richard Nixon. The letter from Nixon thanks Wayne for support while Nixon was vice president.* TOP: *President Gerald Ford (left) and John Wayne share a laugh at a public event.*

CHAPTER SEVEN

FOR THE FANS

"Dear Blazer Class of 1972: I am deeply honored
that you have made me an honorary member.
I am sure you will all develop a code of ethics that
will make me proud to be a member of your class.
Sincerely, John Wayne"

—JOHN WAYNE, RESPONDING TO A LETTER FROM AN
ELEMENTARY SCHOOL CLASS IN NORTH CAROLINA IN 1972

COMMUNICATION WITH HIS FANS WAS FREQUENTLY SHORT, SWEET, AND ENDEARINGLY SIMPLE FOR JOHN WAYNE. When Mrs. Ann Edel of Whittier, California, wrote him in June 1971 just to tell him he was doing a good job, Wayne wanted her to know he appreciated the compliment. "Thank you for your very nice letter," Wayne replied on June 23, 1971. "I will certainly try to keep up the good work, God willing."

That was the entire letter. A year earlier to the day, he responded to a note from Mrs. Daniel Philip Hoover of Massillon, Ohio, regarding her request for an autographed photo. Mrs. Hoover even offered to pay for the picture after telling Wayne about her five children.

"I know you must feel a sense of relief and accomplishment bringing up five children in this day and age," he responded. "That is payment enough for the picture I'm enclosing."

That same week, Wayne dashed off a note to John Smisek of Flushing, Queens, noting his appreciation for the handmade holster Smisek had sent him. "I'll slap a gun into it and give it a try," he promised Mr. Smisek.

Earlier in 1970, Wayne responded to another of several letters from schoolgirl Jenny Lynch of Texarkana, Texas. As usual, he was happy to hear from her.

"Every time I receive a letter from you, the day is brighter," he told Jenny. "You are a very thoughtful little girl, and a much appreciated fan."

A couple months later, while cooped up in a Ramada Inn in Tucson, Arizona, Wayne sent out a flurry of letters to fans and friends on various topics, including thank-you notes to Richard Nixon, J. Edgar Hoover, Lyndon Johnson, and others for their expressions of condolence on the deaths of his mother and brother, and for their congratulations for winning his *True Grit* Academy Award. That week, he also wrote an old classmate, Lee Osborne, then an executive with the Union Pacific Railroad Company, expressing joy on hearing from him; he said he had often wondered what had become of him.

PAGE 108: *John Wayne signs autographs at a Little League baseball game. Wayne typically signed autographs wherever he was, for as long as fans wanted him to. Here, the team ended up being named after him—"the John Wayne Giants."* TOP AND OPPOSITE: *John Wayne poses for pictures with adoring female fans.*

FOR THE FANS

From Richard Nixon to Ann Edel and everyone in between, John Wayne was a serial correspondent with friends, fans, and colleagues alike. Many stacks of letters exist in the John Wayne archive, none taller than the correspondence he maintained with his longtime secretary, Mary St. John (see page 117). Wayne's devotion to communicating with average fans was unwavering, whether the subject was trivial or of crucial importance. For instance, fourteen-year-old Dick Benzie wrote Wayne in August 1972 to tell him he had seen *The Cowboys* and was curious to know where the child actors in the film got their cowboy boots. Wayne promptly supplied the requested information.

"The boys who worked in *The Cowboys* were furnished boots by Western Costume, along with the rest of their wardrobe," he wrote Benzie, before offering another tip. "However, many people buy western boots at Nudies [then located in North Hollywood, California]."

On the other end of the spectrum, in November 1972, a woman named Louise Jackson of Vicksburg, Mississippi, wrote Wayne a heartfelt, six-page letter to tell him that her daughter, Kathy, then almost fifteen years old, had recently had brain surgery and was struggling with her recovery. She wondered if

Wayne might have the time to write her daughter in light of the fact that he had fought through his own dangerous cancer surgery in 1964. Wayne immediately sent Kathy some encouraging words. He described his 1964 cancer ordeal and conceded that recovery was difficult, but achievable.

"Although I still have pain and am short of breath, as the saying goes, 'I've learned to live with it,'" he wrote the young

woman. "I'm one of the lucky ones, for which I thank God every day. Even though our cases are different, I wanted to tell you not to give up. Things have a way of working out."

Indeed, lots of correspondence between Wayne and his fans over the years had to do with the subject of cancer. In May 1969, for example, Herbert Keller of Norristown, Pennsylvania, wrote and asked advice regarding his upcoming cancer operation. Wayne responded by promoting the notion of positive thinking.

"I don't think you'll ever get over feeling some discomfort," he wrote Mr. Keller. "I know that whenever I use certain muscles in my left side, I become very conscious of their position, front and back. But I'm here—and I'm breathing—and I'm happy. Figure you better take the same attitude."

The 1960s coincided with the rise of the antismoking movement. Given Wayne's high profile, his well-known smoking habit, and his 1964 brush with lung cancer, it was natural he would be flooded with requests to speak out against the ills of smoking. Handwritten letters poured in periodically from schoolchildren urging him to stop smoking. After his 1964 cancer surgery, Wayne did quit smoking for a time, but eventually returned to the habit.

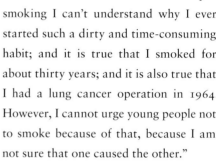

JOHN WAYNE

Wayne politely demurred on such requests—he simply wasn't comfortable with telling people how to live their lives, and he thought such declarations were best left up to scientists and doctors. One time in 1966, he told Mrs. Buford Slover Jr. of Deming, New Mexico, that he could not come to her community and speak out about smoking because of his busy schedule, but also because he wasn't comfortable doing so.

"I have quit smoking and I do think it is a very bad, unattractive habit, but I could not conscientiously make the kind of address you seem to want because I have no way of knowing that smoking brought on my cancer," he explained.

A couple of months later, Montgomery Green of Havre de Grace, Maryland, wrote Wayne at least twice, asking him to share his smoking history and wondering if he could use

Wayne's name as an endorsement for a book Green was writing that linked cigarettes to cancer. Wayne happily shared the tale of how he first got involved with cigarettes, but he again refused to speak out on the subject.

"The first time I can remember smoking was breaking finger firecrackers in two, lighting them at the side, and after a swish of the combustible powder, using one-half the firecracker as a cigarette," Wayne revealed in a May 9, 1966, letter to Mr. Green. "This has a tendency to create a headache, which is not in itself helpful in the promotion of the smoking habit. In spite of this experience, I tried and tried again, until I became what you would most certainly call a habitual cigarette smoker.

"It is true that now that I've quit smoking I can't understand why I ever started such a dirty and time-consuming habit; and it is true that I smoked for about thirty years; and it is also true that I had a lung cancer operation in 1964. However, I cannot urge young people not to smoke because of that, because I am not sure that one caused the other."

Mr. Green asked again in a follow-up letter, but on May 25, 1966, Wayne refused more emphatically, saying, "I can't set myself up and give a sermon on the mount against smoking cigarettes."

He added, "Men who are in a position to know more than you or I about cancer haven't asked for laws to stop cigarette smoking, so it would be presumptuous of me to give out any definitive statements, and I don't intend to do so." Then he thanked Green for his "good citizenship in trying to do something constructive for the national community."

Periodically, people would even write Wayne asking for medical advice. He declined, of course, but routinely offered prayers and well wishes.

OPPOSITE, TOP: *John Wayne signs autographs for fans.* OPPOSITE, BOTTOM: *He poses with the "John Wayne Giants" baseball team with his daughter Aissa.* INSET: *Front and back images of the printed and autographed "good luck" business cards John Wayne frequently carried to hand out to fans when approached in public over the years.*

John Wayne...a Camel fan goin' on 24 years

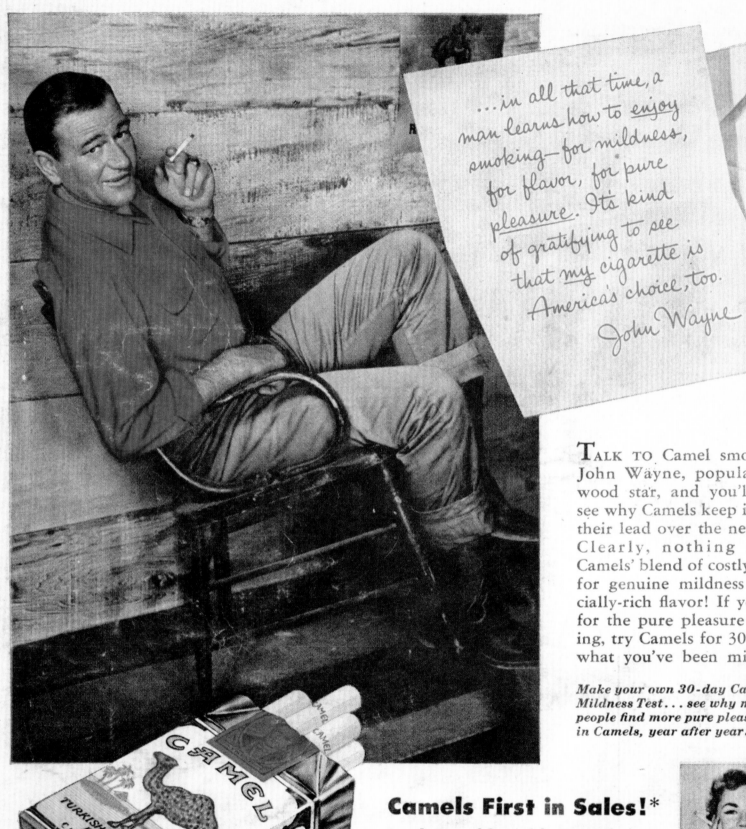

...in all that time, a man learns how to *enjoy* smoking—for mildness, for flavor, for pure pleasure. It's kind of gratifying to see that *my* cigarette is America's choice, too.

John Wayne

TALK TO Camel smokers like John Wayne, popular Hollywood star, and you'll quickly see why Camels keep increasing their lead over the next brand. Clearly, nothing matches Camels' blend of costly tobacco for genuine mildness and specially-rich flavor! If you smoke for the pure pleasure of smoking, try Camels for 30 days. See what you've been missing!

Make your own 30-day Camel Mildness Test... see why more people find more pure pleasure in Camels, year after year!

Camels First in Sales!*
Lead second brand by record

50 8/10 %

* Printers' Ink, 1954

For MILDNESS ...for FLAVOR

Camels agree with more people than any other cigarette!

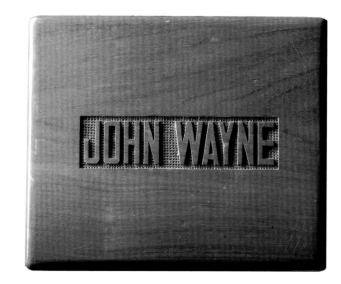

"I'm sorry to hear about your husband," he wrote Mrs. Katherine Ishoy of Chillicothe, Ohio, on April 4, 1968. "His case seems to be much worse than mine. I am unable to advise you as to any medicine, therapy, or treatment of any kind, because I did not have anything like that, either before or after my operation. Sometimes all we can do is hope and pray, and I'm sure you are doing that."

Over the years, Wayne developed an organized and strategic method of corresponding with such fans. Under Mary St. John's direction, secretaries routinely worked in his home for hours each day, simply opening and organizing letters and responses.

"At our house, there were usually at least four secretaries there, answering each piece of fan mail," recalls Wayne's daughter Melinda Wayne Munoz. "He would spend hours sitting at his table, signing his autograph. A large part of his day was correspondence. It was very important to him. He truly loved his fans. He felt that if someone took the time to write him, he should take the time to write him or her back. It meant a lot to people for my dad to take the time to thank them for their letters and sign their pictures, or whatever else he could do for them."

Of course, a chunk of his correspondence involved responding to invitations to events and honors large and small, which he often had to turn down due to his busy schedule. In 1967 and 1968 alone, during the development and making of *The Green Berets*, he sent out dozens of notes offering regrets for not being able to attend a host of events, ranging from Ronald Reagan's gubernatorial inauguration in California to telling the New Trier Township High School student council president that he regretted having no time available to speak at his school.

"It is my hope that through the efforts of men like yourself, the majority of those in your generation will return to the fold of responsible citizenship as soon as the pendulum swings a touch further to the radical left," Wayne told Peterson.

Without question, Wayne was keenly aware of his fame's impact on fans, and he was committed to letting them feel like they had some kind of a personal connection to him. That is why he periodically participated in "at home with the Waynes" newspaper and magazine articles and happily answered when celebrity lifestyle columnists came calling.

For example, Anita Summer, contributing editor of the "Ask Them Yourself" column in *Family Weekly* magazine, wrote Wayne in late October 1975 to ask a few "general interest" questions of the fluffy, lifestyle variety: "How do you avoid overeating at lunch?" "Do you think romance is dead?" "What makes a woman attractive and sexy?" Yet Wayne answered cheerfully.

OPPOSITE: *A Camel cigarette advertisement featuring John Wayne from the 1950s. Wayne smoked most of his life, but never felt comfortable coming out publically against smoking after his 1964 cancer operation, despite repeated requests from advocates.* TOP: *Wayne's engraved cigar box, open and closed.*

The person who corresponded most consistently with John Wayne was Mary St. John—his personal secretary and confidante for more than thirty years. St. John had been in charge of the secretarial pool at Republic Pictures early in his career, and she told journalist Wayne Warga in 1971 that she first met Wayne in 1937 at Republic. In 1946, Wayne offered her a job, and she remained in his employment until her retirement in 1975. Although other secretaries helped her manage Wayne's office over the years, and her handpicked replacement, Pat Stacy, took over the job and became Wayne's companion the last few years of his life, St. John was the glue that kept Wayne's affairs organized during most of his career.

From the 1950s through the early 1970s, St. John would religiously write Wayne when he was out of town making movies or vacationing. Some letters were all business, but others were very personal. Over time, St. John had no compunction about telling Wayne her views about office politics, about the merits of certain projects, and about social or political affairs. Most importantly, she kept him updated about the welfare of his wife, children, and home.

"It was an important relationship—I can't express that strongly enough," says Wayne's son Patrick. "She was a person who worked for him, and yet, it was more than just a job to her. Mary was as dedicated to him as if they were related. She had complete loyalty all those years and was an amazing worker. Mary protected my father. She was a simple little woman, and yet a great and loyal friend to my dad. She had a lot of guts."

St. John's devotion extended to Wayne's entire family and all his interests, and, in fact, she regarded easing his burdens as her primary duty. In a letter on February 20, 1957, after discussing some personality clashes taking place in the Batjac office while Wayne was away, she became confessional about this responsibility.

"In the ten years I have worked for you (I really should say, worked with you, because you have always made me feel that way), I have always approached your problems in a very personal way—as if they were my problems, too," she told him. "I think all of this is so completely understood between us that it is unnecessary for me to go into it further. I've only said this much to remind myself and you that my primary purpose in this job is to help solve as many of the problems that confront you as it is possible for me to solve."

This love and affection was returned by Wayne's family, so much so that Wayne's third wife, Pilar, regards St. John as almost a mother figure in her own life. "She was already working for [Wayne] when he and I met," Pilar remembers. "The two of them were very close. To me, she was more like my mother. She was the maid of honor when we got married, actually."

Mary St. John was particularly concerned about Wayne's travels to remote locations. On January 6, 1956, she wrote, "Please on your next picture consider Griffith Park for the location. I just don't like it when you're so far away. I can't even hear you raising a little hell. Tain't fitting." A year later, on February 25, 1957, she yearned to learn more about a leg injury Wayne had suffered while shooting *Legend of the Lost*, saying, "Libya is just too damn far away and too remote to suit me."

Earlier, on January 2, 1957, she lamented how long he had been away from home. "As I go over the day-to-day calendar, I can't realize it's been another year—that a year ago you were in New York and on your way to Europe for *The Conqueror*, that Aissa wasn't even born, and that by the time you see her again she will be a year old!"

Indeed, many of her letters from this period routinely gave him loving updates on his baby daughter, Aissa, and other children. Though in a February 8, 1957, letter, she concedes: "Haven't seen any of the younger generation—Michael, Patrick, Toni, Melinda, so I guess they are all busy with their individual endeavors. Kids nowadays sure keep busy and occupied. I certainly can't see anything wrong with the younger generation, except perhaps that I'm not part of it."

OPPOSITE: *Mary St. John, longtime secretary and family friend.* INSET: *A short handwritten note from John Wayne to Mary St. John while he was filming in Rome in the late 1950s. The note is typical—he always asked for news from home and from the office and always sent her his love and best wishes.*

On January 15, 1974, John Wayne rode into Cambridge's Harvard Square in an army reserve unit armored personnel carrier ready to "battle" the witty young liberals of *The Harvard Lampoon* and earn, in the process, a little publicity for his new film, *McQ*. The event turned into one of the most enjoyable occasions of Wayne's later life.

"He had a really good time [at Harvard]—those students wanted to murder him politically, and instead, he made them laugh," recalls his daughter Melinda Wayne Munoz. "He was very touched by their interest in him."

The whole thing started when Wayne received a mocking letter from *The Harvard Lampoon* president James Downey urging him to come to Boston and "have it out."

Downey wrote, "You think you're tough? You're not so tough. You have never pored through dozens of critical volumes on imagist poetry. You've never gotten your hands dirty with corrasable bond and corrector fluid...." On and on the sarcastic invitation went: "We dare you to have it out, head on, with the young whelps of Harvard who would call the supposedly unbeatable John Wayne the biggest fraud in history."

Wayne liked the chutzpah of the invitation, and he thought the opportunity to mix it up with bright, sarcastic young people would be fun.

"I accept with pleasure your challenge to bring my new motion picture, *McQ*, into the pseudo-intellectual swamps of Harvard Square," he wrote in reply. "Age, breeding, and political philosophy aside, I am quite prepared to meet nose-to-nose and fact-to-fact any or all of the knee-jerk liberals who foul your campus. Your intellectual pretensions, your pointy headed radicalism, your Mao Tse-Tung quotations, and your high-school French proverbs could hardly pierce the hide of a man who has stormed the Alamo, raised the flag at Iwo Jima, and fought with the Green Berets. So comb out your beards, extinguish your pot and put a book-marker in your Marcuse and Hesse.... I'll be there on Jan. 15 for the premiere of *McQ*, ready to flex muscles with the limpest bunch of baby-brained scholars in America."

On the day of the event, Wayne staged his grand entrance and took questions from Harvard students, thoroughly enjoying a mutual ribbing. When asked if he viewed himself as the fulfillment of the American dream, for instance, he replied, "I don't look at myself more than I have to."

A month later, on February 25, 1974, Wayne wrote Downey to thank him sincerely for the opportunity.

"I take back all the nasty things I thought about the Lampooners," he wrote. "This foothill of a man was thoroughly won over by the Lampooners from the table top in the Castle. Please extend my hearty thanks to all your members for a warm and amusing evening that I shall sadly recall as each of you passes into the next world. In other words, I intend to bury you all."

A banner and medallion presented as gifts to John Wayne by The Harvard Lampoon *at the infamous roasting.*

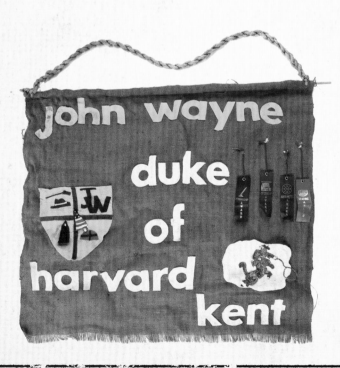

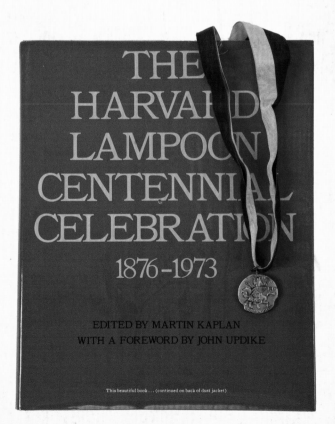

He wrote back: "I don't avoid overeating at lunch," and "I do not think romance is dead. I think there is still puppy love—boy certainly still gets girl—and vice versa for women's lib; and I don't think anything will kill it except one of the two human beings involved. Unlucky for me, my pictures are not loaded with love scenes, but I think it would be quite a task to play them with someone you didn't like."

As to the question about what makes a woman attractive and sexy, he suggested, "They have a pretty good idea without me attempting to tell them."

Wayne was equally gracious when he encountered fans in person. For many years, in fact, he carried autographed business cards around with him that he could pass out when curious fans approached. The cards had Wayne's name printed neatly on the front, and on the back he wrote, "Good luck, John Wayne."

The cards were part of a strategy to be patient and considerate of fans when they encountered or interrupted him, and he always told family members to do likewise. He even tried to understand when such encounters were clearly out of bounds, according to his son Ethan.

"I remember a night [at their home in Newport Beach] when someone was outside making noise," Ethan recalls. "He went out with a flashlight and a small gun and I followed right behind him. It ended up being two marines [on leave] who said they just wanted to say hello. He said, 'Well then, come in and have a drink with me.' He sat down and talked to them and then sent them off and told them, 'Don't ever sneak up on me like that again.'"

Inundated as he was by fan mail, Wayne was bound to encounter criticism in some letters. Like anyone else, he could occasionally be stung by such remarks, and he would sometimes aggressively defend himself or his positions. But if he felt the critique was in earnest, he also took the heartfelt views of others seriously and respectfully.

In October 1969, Mrs. G. W. Sowers Jr. took him to task on a delicate issue for Wayne. He had always avoided using profanity in his films, and finally, in *True Grit*, he allowed his character, Rooster Cogburn, to let fly with a few indelicate words. Mrs. Sowers was not pleased, and she sent Wayne a letter telling him so.

Wayne felt she deserved an explanation.

"I have spent forty years trying to stay within a code of my own which would ensure that anyone of any age could see one of my pictures," he wrote her. "In *True Grit*, I did use the vernacular of the streets but I felt it was so in character with 'Rooster' that it was permissible. Please be assured that in my own way I try to keep pictures healthy enough for the whole family to see." ✪

TOP: *In Hawaii, sailors enjoy some time drinking with John Wayne and getting autographs from their legendary visitor.*

FRIENDS

AND

FUN

"There was his on-screen life and his public life, and then there was his private life. It was the private life where he was most relaxed and comfortable."

—PATRICK WAYNE

JOHN WAYNE LIVED FOR MANY YEARS IN NEWPORT BEACH, but in a sense, his real home was his yacht, *Wild Goose*. According to his son Ethan, it was "the one place where he could relax and get away from all the obligations he had to deal with" as a public figure. Wayne's daughter Marisa adds that the boat was "the place where he would always go to recharge his batteries."

"He'd dive for abalone," Ethan reminisces. "He'd dive for lobster. He'd fish. He played cards and chess all day long. He went swimming and sat in the sun, just relaxing in Mexico. I remember him putting on his shirt and a pair of flip-flops and just jumping over the side and swimming to shore in some remote Mexican village. When he got there, he'd be all wet and would just have something to eat or a drink, talk to people, and then swim back and hang out with his buddies."

Indeed, John Wayne would routinely take family and friends on the *Wild Goose* to places like Mexico, Alaska, British Columbia, Catalina, and many others. Wayne bought the yacht in 1962 after owning a smaller boat for a few years.

"When I was younger, he owned a boat called the *Norwester*," recalls his son Patrick. "We had a lot of fun, but it wasn't big enough with our huge extended family, so eventually he decided to buy the *Wild Goose*."

PAGE 120: *Deep-sea fishing was one of John Wayne's many outdoor-related passions.* TOP: *Wayne and oldest son Michael haul lobsters out of the ocean during one of their many diving excursions over the years.* RIGHT: *Wayne and Michael also tried their hand at spearfishing.* OPPOSITE, TOP LEFT: *Boating adventures began long before the* Wild Goose *came along.* OPPOSITE, TOP RIGHT: *Wayne deep-sea fishing with his youngest son, Ethan.* OPPOSITE, BOTTOM: *Wayne and family and friends enjoying a cruise, diving, and relaxing onboard his first yacht, the* Norwester.

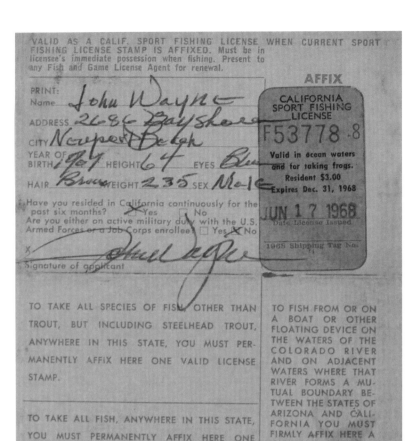

for example. He developed the story for *The Green Berets* during regular meetings on the boat during those years, and he took out friends ranging from Jack Valenti and Lynda Bird Johnson to Dean Martin and Barry Goldwater, among others.

The one-hundred-and-thirty-six-foot *Wild Goose* had been a US Navy minesweeper during World War II. After the war, it was converted into a private yacht, and its second owner, Max Wyman of Seattle, eventually sold it to John Wayne in 1962. In a September 5, 1962, letter to Wayne while preparing the boat

for transfer of ownership, Wyman recommended he hire British citizen Ken Minshall as his chief engineer, which Wayne did. The following year, when an opening came up in the boat's six-man crew, Minshall recommended his brother, Bert Minshall, to serve as a deckhand, and Bert joined the *Wild Goose* while it was cruising between Europe and Mexico.

In his book about his years on the *Wild Goose* and in an interview for this book, Minshall has fondly discussed first meeting Wayne when the boat was docked in La Paz, Mexico.

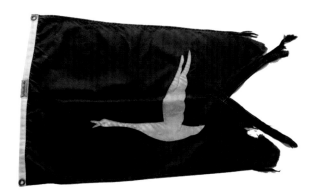

TOP: *Stern view of the* Wild Goose *flying its flag and off on another cruise.* BOTTOM LEFT: *The* Wild Goose *nautical flag.* OPPOSITE: *Fishing adventures were almost a yearly ritual for John Wayne.* OPPOSITE, TOP: *Checking the catch with his friends Ernie Saftig and Andy Devine, and son Patrick Wayne.* OPPOSITE, BOTTOM LEFT: *The Minshall brothers, Bert (left) and Ken (right), with John and Ethan Wayne.* OPPOSITE, BOTTOM RIGHT: *Marisa, Ethan, John Wayne, Patrick, and Pete Stein.*

He was shocked when the legendary star suddenly spit on his new deck shoes.

"He put a hand on my shoulder and said, 'Bert, always spit on new shoes for good luck,'" Minshall explains today. "That was my introduction to the great John Wayne. He liked me because I took good care of his children. It was easily the best job I ever had."

Bert Minshall rose from deckhand to first mate to, eventually, captain of the boat, but in those early days, his primary job was to keep an eye on Wayne's three young children. Minshall affectionately recalls having fun with them on board the *Wild Goose*, like "water skiing and jumping off John Wayne's cabin, about 25 feet in the air. And then, about 4 o'clock each day, the kids would get tired and we would play a game or watch TV or just relax with a soda and watch the sun go down. Duke did use the boat until late in life, but never so much as when his kids were little. He loved taking them out on that boat."

Soon after joining the crew, Minshall was promoted to first mate after a terrible tragedy in Mexico resulted in the deaths of three deckhands. The trio died in March 1964 after receiving permission to go ashore and take a taxi to a party. Instead, they and a fourth crewman attempted to reach the fiesta in the small skiff that was supposed to be used only to get them to shore. In

there is a letter to a lawyer in Mexico from one of Wayne's attorneys, Frank Belcher, a few weeks after the incident, indicating how badly Wayne felt about the tragedy. The letter instructed the attorney to arrange some financial assistance for the widow of the married crewman who had perished. The letter states, "John feels not the slightest responsibility in connection with the death of this boy, but he does want to do something for the [widow]."

Most of the years Wayne owned the *Wild Goose*, the boat's skipper was a crusty, opinionated sea salt named Pete Stein. Judging from archival letters, Stein was rather friendly with his boss, "even though they would fight like cats and dogs, and then make up," according to Ethan Wayne.

"They argued over all sorts of things, but it was clear they liked each other," Ethan adds. "They would sometimes drink together—never during the day or when the boat was in operation, but at night. Typically, we would be full of activity all day. Swimming, playing cards, sunning, hiking, fishing, or exploring, and then maybe diving or something like that. Then, the sun would set, and we would have a nice dinner, and then the adults would have cocktails. But by the next morning, everyone was up early, we'd all have to pitch in to clean the boat, do some exercise, maybe go into town for supplies, and then it would all start again."

the choppy late-night waters, the skiff overturned and three of the young men were lost.

Minshall had originally planned to join them before changing his mind. He recalls Wayne and his family being "totally devastated that night." No wrongdoing was involved or implied—it was simply a tragic accident. In the Wayne archives

When Wayne was away from the boat, Stein would periodically send letters updating him on the vessel, its charter schedule, and other things. They were fond letters addressed to "Duke" and always signed "Skipper." When Wayne was out of the country on a shoot in late 1967, Stein wrote him on October 13 and expressed a yearning for his boss to rejoin his crew.

John Wayne's tough-guy image takes a hit when one reads the stream of emotional comments he made about his mentor and dear friend John Ford over the years. From the time they became close when Wayne was trying to break into the motion picture business in the 1920s (see page 33) until Ford's death in 1973, the two men behaved as if they were blood kin. Wayne always kept a framed, autographed portrait of Ford prominently displayed in his home, and by many accounts, he would often defer to the famous and sometimes persnickety director even after becoming the world's biggest star.

"Ford took a special liking to me which gradually grew into a very fine manly love," Wayne explained in his unfinished biography about his relationship with the man he usually called "Pappy," "Coach," or "Jack."

One of the notable things about their personal letters is the frequent, almost unrelenting use of nicknames, inside jokes, and silly teasing that might typify any collegial relationship between two old buddies. On November 4, 1949, Wayne addressed a letter to Ford: "My Dear Mr. Ford; and/or Bull Feeney." The letter appears to relate to the fact that Ford was planning to attend a football game. Wayne, a bit more experienced in gridiron matters, sent Ford a series of "rules" regarding football etiquette.

ABOVE: *John Wayne (left) listens as his friend, colleague, and mentor, John Ford, holds court.* OPPOSITE: *A few lighthearted notes from Wayne to Ford from over the years, out of dozens.*

"Inasmuch as there's no camera there, you're not supposed to tell the players what to do," he wrote, and later cautioned him, "at the end of the game, please leave all blankets as you find them. Yours is at home in your den, with the ladies' dress forms, sewing machines, old drapes, and black and tan tams."

Wayne also sent Ford postcards from faraway locales and wrote little jokes on the back regarding the photograph on the front. In 1955, he sent a postcard from Germany that pictured a Bavarian beer hall. On the back, John Wayne hand-scrawled, "You can't get D-R-U-N-K on beer. Mark Twain."

When Wayne's home caught fire in 1958 while he was filming in Japan, he sent Ford a simple telegram to fill him in on what happened. "It's nothing really—house burned down," he exaggerated. "Found portrait of [Ward] Bond but [stuntman and friend Frank] McGrath's nose is missing. Love, Duke."

On and on the kibitzing went. In a February 25, 1957, note, Ford wrote to Wayne, who was shooting overseas, ostensibly to update him on his family, since Ford was spending more time with them than Wayne was. Characteristically, the director couldn't resist tweaking his old friend.

"I called [your] house and the baby is fine—she is calling Ward [Bond] 'Papa,'" Ford wrote. "Also [Wayne's dog] Sampson is improving and biting your milkman."

Such joking makes clear that the affection between the two men ran deep and was mutual. Occasionally, though, they put the joking aside. On December 7, 1955, Ford wrote Wayne, who was trying to decide whether to do a project with a different director. Ford's primary concern was that Wayne not feel obligated to him.

"God knows I want you for the picture, but you mustn't do it as a sacrifice to yourself," Ford wrote. "You have been doing that for me for too many years. If you have any chance for a great deal, please be assured that I understand perfectly. After all, nothing ain't never going to break up our friendship."

Indeed, nothing ever did break it up. When John Ford passed away in 1973, in fact, close friends of both men sent sympathy cards to John Wayne like any other family member. That week, Wayne told the *Burbank Daily Review* newspaper that he went to see Ford the day before he died and that "the man was my heart. There was a communion between us that not many men have. I have never been closer to any person in my life than I have been with Jack."

November 4, 1949

Mr. John Ford,
Argosy Productions,
Culver City, Calif.

My Dear Mr. Ford:
 and/or
Bull Feeney:

Due to the fact that you haven't had the experience
of sitting on benches that "Judge" Bond and I have
had, I think you might find these rules very helpful:

(a). You're not allowed to enter the playing field
     without the permission of the coach - Cravath,
     that is.

(b). Inasmuch as there's no camera there, you're not
     supposed to tell the players what to do.

(c). At the end of the game, please leave all
     blankets as you find them. Yours is at home
     in your den, with the ladies' dress forms,
     sewing machines, old drapes, and black and
     tan tams.

(d). If you can get your hands on a helmet and
     noseguard, please bring same for Grant to
     wear at the next bridge game.

(e). The stock company is full. Kindly refrain
     from signing up anyone for stunts or props.

(f). Speaking of stunts, at half-time you will
     hear them call for stunts. Don't be surprised
     when Kennedy, Lyons and Post Parks don't come
     forward. They do it with cards, so you won't
     need Lowell to make a deal with them.

(g). Steponovitch might be in the stands, so look
     out if it's a muddy field.

(h). Please take notice that none of the "kids"
     are playing the game anymore.

(i). In order to save a thousand words, we have
     enclosed a picture. This is where you
     might be of great service, as you understand
     thoroughly how to handle "you-know-whats".

(j). It is not considered ethical to switch benches
     if the other team is winning.

(k). Last - but not least - please do not destroy
     the bearer of this letter.

                    In hoc,

P.S. I did not type this letter - it was done
     by a Public Stenographer.

"I haven't really seen much of the family but from all reports they are well, but evidently lonesome and impatient for your return, as is the *Wild Goose* crew," Stein wrote. "Truthfully, the boys and I miss you around the boat and hope you can get back soon to enjoy it."

Wayne was strongly loyal to his "boys" on the boat. In February 1966, he demonstrated that loyalty when the *Wild Goose* brushed up against another yacht during a trip to Catalina when Wayne was not on board. The owner of the other yacht, though conceding his boat was barely damaged, wrote Wayne a long letter claiming that Captain Stein was less than cooperative during the incident—calling Stein "arrogant."

TOP: *Patrick Wayne (left) joins his father and Ernie Saftig (right) and a crew member on a boating excursion.* OPPOSITE, TOP: *Arriving in Hawaii, the Wayne clan leaves the airport and heads out on another vacation. Such group trips were common in those years.* OPPOSITE, BOTTOM: *One of dozens of unopened bottles of wine, and other liquors, left behind by John Wayne and still sitting in the John Wayne archives today. People around the world routinely sent Wayne bottles, cases, and cartons of wine and other spirits, which he usually kept on board the* Wild Goose, *but at his death, dozens of cases remained unopened.*

Wayne wrote the man back a couple weeks later, quite displeased by the accusation.

"[Stein] recalls nothing discourteous in his actions, and says he took a ten-minute lecture from you without anger or reply," Wayne wrote. "It is unfortunate that the incident occurred, but I can't feel that anything that happened gives you license to damn me and my ship and crew as arrogant. Quite frankly, the tone of your letter fails to invoke a sympathetic or apologetic attitude from me."

Wayne, of course, had other outlets for social fun when he was on land. His iconic status earned him invitations and memberships of all types that he wasn't shy about using when he could. He was, for instance, a member of the Newport Harbor Yacht Club, the Playboy Club, a Knott's Berry Farm Gold Season Pass holder, a member of the Colt Commemorative Gun Collector's Association of America, the Yacht Club of Acapulco, the Royal Order of Jesters, and the Mount Kenya Safari Club—founded by his friend, actor William Holden—among other organizations.

Over the years, Wayne's family routinely enjoyed traveling to movie locations, big Thanksgiving parties at the 26 Bar Ranch,

industry events, and much more. Still, like anyone else, much of his greatest joy revolved around simple, old-fashioned family time, particularly in the years he lived in Newport Beach with his third wife, Pilar, and three youngest children, Aissa, Ethan, and Marisa (for more on Wayne's family, see Chapter Nine).

In fact, the *Wild Goose* was the prime reason why he eventually moved his family in 1965 from Encino, in the heart of the San Fernando Valley in Los Angeles, to Newport Beach, where he docked the boat. Family members say, for health reasons, he also wanted to get away from the polluted air of Los Angeles. The Waynes moved into a spacious ranch house on Bayshore Drive in Newport Beach, where, when they were young, the Wayne children recall living a fairly typical life, similar to any other large family—if one discounts the massive volume of fan mail arriving daily, requiring secretaries to work at the home to sort through it all (see page 115), and Wayne's periodic lengthy absences to go make movies. Otherwise, the daily routine involved lots of chess, cards, and board games; big dinners with family and friends; station wagon trips to the hardware store,

the drug store, and the supermarket; plus chores, home maintenance, and loads of school work.

Wayne's office/den, where he had a projection system installed, was a frequent gathering site for "movie night at the Waynes," and not just to watch John Wayne movies. For many years, he borrowed copies of new feature films from his contacts at studios and invited friends and family to watch them—an always popular event at the family home. On November 11, 1977, for example, the Waynes and their friends gathered to watch *Star Wars* and *Heroes* in the den, and on March 10, 1978, they enjoyed a triple feature—*Annie Hall, Smokey and the Bandit,* and *High Anxiety.*

The Waynes routinely hosted, attended, and enjoyed parties large and small, of course, and elaborate Wayne Christmas parties were an annual affair for many years. Without question, John Wayne loved a good party and a nice drink, something he didn't try to deny or hide.

Indeed, when famed film critic Roger Ebert published a feature article about Wayne's visit to Chicago in the *Chicago Sun-Times* on September 12, 1976,

Wayne wrote to Ebert's editors to complain about the tenor of the article. He insisted he no longer smoked cigars, as Ebert wrote, but he freely confirmed his drinking preferences.

"As far as the tequila is concerned, I certainly did drink it," he wrote. "I prefer it to, say, a scotch and soda. For humor, I told [Ebert] the story of tequila never giving you a hangover but that you had to watch your back because you fall down a lot."

In many of his adventures over the years, Wayne was frequently joined by his closest friends. John Ford was the closest—a combination father figure/kindred spirit. Their mutual devotion has been well documented over the years, as well as their lengthy professional association. In fact, their personal letters tell a tender tale of true and meaningful friendship.

And Wayne wasn't shy about admitting it. In October 1971, he replied to an inquiry from the Italian magazine *L'Europeo* by declaring, "John Ford, 'Pappy' to a great many people of my generation, has been a guiding force in my life for forty years.

Not only is he my mentor in my work, but he has been important in the development of whatever character I have."

Wayne typically signed his letters to Ford with either the salutation "affectionately" or "your everlovin'." The letters are filled with inside jokes, teasing references, silly nicknames, and innuendo that probably no one other than the two of them would ever fully understand (for more from their letters, see page 126).

On February 2, 1949, for instance, Wayne sent Ford a note with a belated birthday greeting, telling him, "I didn't think I would ever receive final and conclusive proof that your ass is really out—at my expense." Then he cryptically signed it from "Merriwell (Frank, the Brave One)," probably a reference to a dime-novel hero.

Such birthday greetings flew back and forth between the two men over the decades, with the recurring theme being "out on your ass." On January 26, 1953, for instance, Wayne sent Ford a card congratulating him on his forty-second birthday in

which he wrote, "the last few lines of our traditional birthday song: 'We're flat on our ass, our room rent is due, but never mind about us, Happy Birthday to you.'"

The only hint of friction between them that ever surfaces in any of the available letters appears to be Ford's occasional

OPPOSITE: *Aerial view of John Wayne's Bayshore Drive home in Newport Beach, California, where he and his family spent the last 14 years of his life.* TOP LEFT: *Christmas was always a major event in the Wayne household. John Wayne celebrates with his youngest children (Ethan, with his father, Marisa, left, and Aissa) at their Newport Beach home.* TOP RIGHT: *Ethan Wayne revels in the Christmas overflow as an adolescent.* BOTTOM: *Wayne celebrates his 70th birthday with family and friends.*

BLACKIE AND THE FIRE

On January 15, 1958, Mary St. John sent John Wayne, then filming in Japan, a long, heartfelt update on his family following a major fire in the Wayne home. Pilar Wayne was woken by her dog, Blackie, as the house filled with smoke—a turn of events that made the newspapers—and St. John was full of praise for the little creature.

"Well, I can't say the smoke has cleared, because it hasn't, and probably won't for many, many months," she began the letter. "But the shock and relief of finding everyone safe and uninjured after all those frantic telephone calls at three o'clock in the morning and that awful blaze that greeted us as we neared the house, that has minimized everything else. Thank God of little Blackie, as Pilar was sound asleep and had been for several hours. We sure got that little dog a big, beautiful hunk of roast beef and all the coffee he wanted."

The family dog Blackie, who woke Pilar when a fire broke out in their home in 1958 while Wayne was shooting a movie in Japan.

---

irritation when he could not readily get John Wayne on the phone. In each instance, Wayne was keenly sensitive to Ford's feelings.

On April 20, 1961, Wayne wrote Ford to apologize for not coming to the phone. He stated, "I talk to every Tom, Dick, and Harry who calls. I certainly would not be too tired to talk to a man whom I consider my best friend—that I have a feeling of blood kinship with. But the hell with that—you know it's not true."

A little over a year later, on May 28, 1963, a similar incident occurred, and Wayne took up the "Tom, Dick, and Harry" theme again, even addressing the letter to Ford that way. He was eager to explain that, this time, it was all a big misunderstanding while his wife was asleep.

"Pilar understood [housekeeper] Consuelo to say that Barbara Ford was calling her, so she said she would call her back," he explained to his friend. "That's why I never got the call from Tom, Dick, and Harry. Don't pretend I'm ducking you," he added.

When it happened again in 1966, John Wayne simply apologized in a June 9 letter, writing, "I've been irresponsible for someone I really love. Please forgive me, Coach."

Wayne and Ford were often joined in their adventures by their other old-time pal, actor Ward Bond, whose sudden death in 1960 left a void that Wayne lamented for years.

Bond was a hard-drinking raconteur and character actor in Hollywood whose politics made the conservative Wayne look like

an ultra-progressive. But from the moment they met—on that cross-country train trip in 1929 to film the early Ford football picture *Salute* (see page 33)—they became the closest of friends.

Ward Bond references dot the Wayne-Ford letters from the 1950s. On July 8, 1953, Wayne, on location in Mexico working with Bond on *Hondo*, wrote Ford and reported that, "even Bond looks good."

"After seven years he has even given up saccharine," Wayne added. "Mary [St. John] explained to him that it was bad for the manly qualities in a male. It evidently enlightened him on a subject about which he was having a recent weakness, because he dropped the bottle as if it were a rabbi's knife."

Beyond Ford and Bond, several other dear friends routinely popped up in Wayne's activities and letters over the years. They range from his ranching partner, Louis Johnson, to director Henry Hathaway and actor Harry Carey Jr. (son of his former colleague and cowboy acting idol), to actress and costar Maureen O'Hara and screenwriter Jimmy Grant, among others.

Wayne's relationship with O'Hara and her husband, Charles Blair, blossomed as they starred in five pictures together, took cruises on the *Wild Goose*, and hosted their respective families at a wide range of gatherings over time. Blair was a famous pilot who enjoyed playing chess with Wayne. O'Hara, in several interviews, has fondly recalled evenings making dinner for both men—frequently steak and potatoes, by request.

KNICKKNACKS

The John Wayne archives are filled with old-fashioned, dog-eared catalogues, marked up by John Wayne as he pored through them, hunting for interesting treasures to purchase by mail order. The archives also contain many of these very items and others Wayne picked up during his travels. He was, in fact, a voracious shopper and collector, according to his family.

"Wherever we went, he was buying things—going to little shops," Ethan Wayne explains. "And he loved to buy things out of catalogues. I'm not sure exactly what his motivation was, but he certainly loved to shop."

In addition to his collection of Native American kachina dolls, guns, Western art, and the like (see Chapter Three), Wayne actively collected rocks and seashells from his travels, and he routinely took his wife, Pilar, to buy expensive antiques in far-off locations like London, Japan, the Middle East, and other places. "I used to tell him he was really a frustrated interior decorator with all his art," Pilar chuckles today.

Indeed, a quick look through some of the boxes in the John Wayne archives will tell you that. At the time of his death, John Wayne had procured such disparate items as a mountain lion sculpture by artist James Thomas Turner Sr., a two-hundred-year-old porcelain famille rose flower pot, a hundred-year-old Chinese porcelain yellow vase shaped like a chicken, a fourteen-karat-gold Dunhill lighter, a hundred-dollar whaling harpoon from Massachusetts, a Revolutionary War limited edition chess set, a series of "Lucky 4-Leaf Clover" paperweights, a brass coffee urn, a Brown Bess musket from the British American Bicentennial Group in Philadelphia, a Chinese planter from the Denver Art Museum, and much more. Pictured on this page are just a few of the items he purchased over the years.

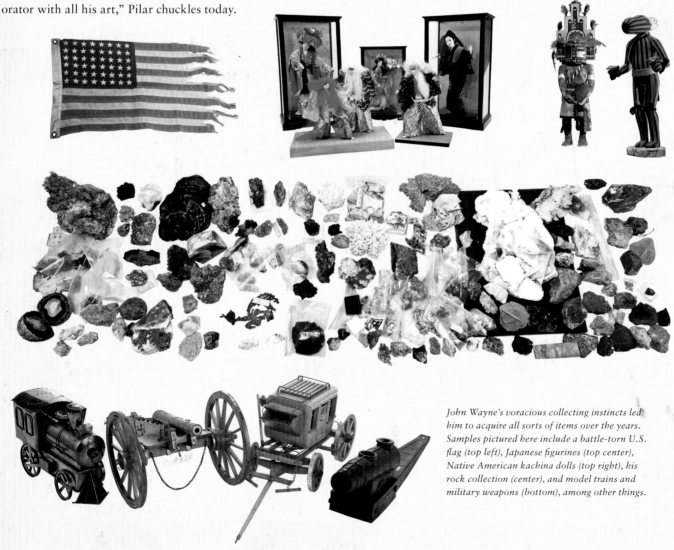

John Wayne's voracious collecting instincts led him to acquire all sorts of items over the years. Samples pictured here include a battle-torn U.S. flag (top left), Japanese figurines (top center), Native American kachina dolls (top right), his rock collection (center), and model trains and military weapons (bottom), among other things.

Over the years, O'Hara has referred to her relationship with Wayne as being of the "brother-sister variety" despite their famous on-screen romantic chemistry, which often led fans to presume they were romantically involved. On the subject of her old friend, she often references Wayne getting "misty eyed" or "dewy eyed" about his kids, friends, and particular memories.

Jimmy Grant was a close professional collaborator with Wayne, having written original stories and/or screenplays for twelve of Wayne's films. The archives contain numerous letters from Grant, writing not only to John Wayne, but also sometimes to Wayne and his wife, Pilar, and sometimes to Mary St. John— discussing everything from business concerns to their mutual health issues. In fact, on November 3, 1964, following a letter of concern from Grant, John Wayne wrote him back and graphically detailed his recent cancer operation.

"They took out something between the size of a golf ball and a baseball—and said the operation was successful," Wayne wrote to his friend. "Then I coughed and broke some ribs and started coughing air into my system at regular intervals, causing such edema that when I pushed up on my face you could hear the air going 'swish' as it was going out. So, five days later they went in along the same trail and sewed up my lung, and said I was fine again, which I guess I am. But it still hurts like Billy-be-damned because of the steadiness of the pain."

Maureen O'Hara suggests Wayne's dedication to these friends, and many others, was largely due to Wayne's intense sense of loyalty, which endured through thick and thin. Indeed, when speaking to Congress urging the creation of a John Wayne commemorative medal in 1979 (see page 101), O'Hara publicly declared this to be Wayne's only glaring fault.

"He is cursed with one failing, his loyalty to friends," she stated. "And it has cost him many sad moments and many happy moments. But he will never cease to be loyal, ever."

Through it all, though, especially late in life, John Wayne's heart never moved far from his beloved *Wild Goose*. It was fortuitous that he was able to take one final cruise to Catalina on the boat during the waning days of his cancer battle in 1979.

Bert Minshall says that final cruise took place on Easter weekend in April 1979, just days after Wayne's final public appearance on the 1979 Academy Awards telecast. Minshall wrote in his book, *On Board with the Duke*, and reiterated in an interview for this book, that Wayne was particularly thin, gaunt, and tired. He was unable to even complete a short, familiar hike on Catalina—a place where, years before, "he'd raised hell with friends like Ward Bond, [actor] Vic McLaglen, and Pappy Ford." But he nevertheless enjoyed spirited games of backgammon and gin rummy and reminisced with several friends during the weekend.

"It was his final trip—he had already talked about selling the boat," Minshall says today. "When we got back and he walked up the dock—that was the last time I saw him. I think it was a happy weekend for him—I certainly hope so." ✪

CHAPTER NINE

FAMILY MOMENTS

"Maybe, to give hope to someone who has cancer....
If I can help some poor devil—or at least give
him hope—then I'm repaid enough."
—JOHN WAYNE, IN A *San Antonio Express* INTERVIEW, MARCH 14, 1965

E THAN WAYNE WAS SEVENTEEN AND LIVING WITH HIS DAD IN THEIR NEWPORT BEACH HOME on May 1, 1979, when John Wayne got off a phone call with his doctor, wearily entered his room, and said, "Come on, you have to take me to the hospital." Ethan drove his dad to the UCLA Medical Center in Los Angeles, about sixty miles up the freeway. The boy had never driven a car as far as Los Angeles, but he knew it was serious or his dad never would have made such a request.

"I remember him getting into the back of our station wagon and laying down," Ethan recalls. "He would normally have never let me drive on my own, but he wasn't feeling well. That's what I remember being shocked about. I figured out how to get there. But as we drove, I didn't realize he would never leave the hospital."

It was a difficult period, understandably, for the Wayne family. But it was also a period that produced some of their most passionate and loving memories of their father. Their dad, they all say, worked hard to express how much he loved them, even as he continued courageously fighting late-stage cancer.

His youngest daughter, Marisa Wayne, however, does recall a moment when her dad reluctantly conceded his fate to her one day in the hospital. She was just thirteen.

Marisa remembers, "He kept saying, 'I hate to leave you, baby, I hate to leave you, I just want to see you marry a good guy. I want to live long enough to see you marry a good guy.' I kept telling him I'd be fine. I didn't realize how sick he really was until then."

Marisa offered these remembrances while cradling a picture of her dad, hastening to add that he was "funny, with a great sense of humor. He had real charisma—he was a genuine bright light in this world."

Such memories of John Wayne's final days contextualize the depth of his impact on those close to him—an impact that reverberates to this day. While the rest of the world viewed him as an icon, to the Wayne children, John Wayne was, as Marisa noted, "just a really great dad."

"He had a real passion for his kids," adds her mother, Pilar. "When we got married, I had been an actress, and Duke told

PAGE 136: *Fatherly embrace for oldest daughter Toni.* TOP: *John Wayne lets daughter Aissa (in back) and baby granddaughters Anita LaCava (now Anita LaCava Swift) and Alicia Wayne explore his office.* OPPOSITE: *John Wayne's first four children line up for a photo. Left to right: Michael, Toni, Patrick, and Melinda.*

139

me we did not have to have kids. But I wanted kids, and he was so happy. He was so sweet with them. He would do anything for them."

Raising a family is something John Wayne did twice, and in both cases, he strove to keep his children close despite his globetrotting schedule. In 1933, at the age of twenty-six, Wayne married Josephine Saenz. Their marriage only lasted until 1945, but by then, Josephine had given him four children—Michael, Toni, Patrick, and Melinda. Josephine remained in her children's lives, and stayed quietly out of the limelight, until her death in 2003. The four older Wayne children were young when their parents divorced, and yet, according to their daughter Melinda Wayne Munoz, her parents maintained cordial relations for decades while cooperating on parenting responsibilities.

"My mother and father were very respectful to one another and never spoke against each other," Melinda says today. "That is a great example of how two people can be parents even though they are not married. My mom never gave an interview or talked about him [after their divorce], and he was hugely respectful and appreciative of her. We lived with my mom and spent summers with him. He was already established [in the film business], and his approach was pretty traditional—he usually went along with what she wanted in raising us. But they were both adamant about school and knew education was the key to life.

"My mother was the one who taught us how to act in public, and she made it very clear that we had to act [responsibly]. She told us to remember, if you sneak into a movie theater with your friends and get caught, you will end up in the newspaper because you are John Wayne's daughter."

Melinda and her brother Patrick—the two surviving children from Wayne's first marriage—emphasize that the two Wayne families were always close. Melinda recalls an episode near the end of her father's life, when he took her and her half sister Marisa—Wayne's youngest daughter—to British Columbia on the *Wild Goose* on a fishing trip in 1977. Wayne was having heart problems by then, and he was also close to entering his

STATE OF CALIFORNIA   COUNTY OF LOS ANGELES

CERTIFICATE OF MARRIAGE

I Hereby Certify that on the ___24th___ day of ___June___ 19_33_,
at ___Los Angeles___, in the County of Los Angeles, State of California,
under authority of a license issued by L. E. Lampton, County Clerk of said County, I, the
undersigned, as a Priest Pastor Church of the Immaculate Conception, joined in marriage,
___Marion Mitchell Morrison___ and ___Josephine Alicia Saenz___,
in the presence of ___S. Gerpheide___, residing at ___San Diego___,
California, and ___Loretta Young___, residing at ___Bel Air___,
California, who witnessed the ceremony.

___Francis J. Conaty___
Signature of person solemnizing marriage

I Hereby Certify that the foregoing is a copy of the
original certificate of marriage of the parties therein named.

___Francis J. Conaty___
Signature of person solemnizing marriage

My darling Lissa

It was wonderful to hear your voice last night. Your dad is an especially lucky fellow to have a daughter like you. Every day you are growing into a more gentle little lady. I am very proud of you. Sorry you can't come to this location but I know you will not mind if mommie joins me for a few days visit. Thank you for making me a proud and happy father.

Affectionately

Daddy

P.S. Don't forget the stars.

final battle with cancer, but he decided to hike with his two daughters to a waterfall.

"We got about halfway there, and he said he was pooped," Melinda recalls. "He told us to keep going, and he turned back to [return to the boat]. I remembered thinking for a moment, having a feeling as I saw him walking away, what if he didn't make it? What if he died? That was the first time I ever felt that way. And Marisa felt the same way. When we came back on board the ship, we saw him instead on the ground playing with five or six native children and having a great time. It was so adorable. Instead of worrying about how he felt, he was enjoying his time. Marisa and I were half-sisters, but we were very close and felt exactly the same things. He taught us that—to love your family and keep them close."

After divorcing Josephine in December 1945, Wayne married Esperanza Baur in January 1946. Theirs was a short, turbulent, childless marriage that fell apart quickly—they separated in 1952—but it took several years of painful, and sometimes public,

wrangling to officially terminate. But on the day his divorce from Esperanza was finalized, November 1, 1954, he immediately married Pilar Pallete, who remained his wife until his death, although they eventually separated in 1973.

Wayne met Pilar in 1953, after separating from Esperanza, during a visit to the set of a local movie she was making in her native Peru. They became friendly, and a couple months later, when Pilar came to Hollywood to work on dubbing that same movie from Spanish into English, she ran into him again. They began dating, waited a year until his divorce was finalized, and then married in Kona, Hawaii, while Wayne was filming *Sea Chase*.

OPPOSITE, TOP LEFT: *Beaming new dad John Wayne with baby Patrick.* OPPOSITE, BOTTOM LEFT: *More hugs for daughter Marisa (left) and granddaughter Laura Muñoz.* OPPOSITE, RIGHT: *Wayne takes daughters Toni (left), Melinda (on shoulder), and son Patrick on an outing.* TOP: *Aissa peruses her father's script from the director's chair on the set of* The Alamo.

JOHN WAYNE

Pilar gave him three children—Aissa, Ethan, and Marisa. Pilar shared Wayne's life at the pinnacle of his fame and involvement on the national stage, and she remains deeply moved by the adventure they went on together over those years. To this day, she says, "No one I ever met could touch John Wayne."

"When we married, I knew his style of living, that it would be hard for two people to be in the movies in the same family, plus we both wanted children," Pilar explains. "So we had three children, and I went to every location for every movie he made. I would go ahead, rent a house, try to get him a king-size bed, and arrange things the way he liked them."

Pilar adds that John Wayne "never wanted to live in Beverly Hills or Bel Air, or have movie stars around him all the time. He wanted to live where we could have acreage and be near his boat, so we moved to Newport Beach."

Over the years, though, John and Pilar Wayne grew apart and finally separated in 1973, although they remained married. Today, Pilar suggests their separation was not about their love for one another, nor about any particular event or incident. Rather, she says, "it was a lot of little things put together. We just kind of faded apart after about twenty years together. But to the bitter end, we remained good friends."

Pilar says her pursuit of her own career and interests, combined with Wayne's travel and the pressure of life with a global star, all pushed her in other directions to the point where they split up. "I opened a little restaurant and had an interior design place, and at that time in my life, I wanted to do something more than just follow him all over the world," she says. "I loved being his wife but also wanted to be something more myself."

Finally, she adds, Wayne's ongoing battle with smoking, and her concern about what it was doing to his health, also drove a wedge between them.

"We smoked together for many years—almost everyone did in those days," she recalls. "I eventually quit smoking. But he kept smoking, and there was no stopping him. He abused cigarettes terribly and couldn't stop. He wouldn't use a match—he would light a new cigarette with the old one. When he took a drag, it was with all his heart. That was a real shame and quite an ordeal.

OPPOSITE: *Pilar Palette entertains and chats with John Wayne during their very first meeting in Peru in 1952. They married two years later and raised three children together.* TOP LEFT: *Pilar and John Wayne dressed for a night out.* TOP RIGHT: *John Wayne waits for his wife, Pilar, to get ready. They were married from 1954 until his death, although they separated near the end of his life.*

I remember when he really started to cough in 1964 after making *In Harm's Way* in Hawaii. When he got home, [he went to] Scripps Clinic to check it out. That is when they found the spot on his lung, and he had surgery immediately. The doctor told him that if he didn't smoke for the next eight years, he'd beat it."

During that period, Pilar says, her husband did his best to avoid smoking and told people he had "conquered cancer."

"But then we went to a fancy party in San Francisco, and when I turned around, I saw him with a cigarette in his hand," she remembers. "I was very upset. I didn't like it—it was part of the reason we separated. But that was the only real problem between us—I always loved him and wanted what was best for him."

After the couple split up, Wayne turned for companionship to his new secretary, Pat Stacy, who replaced Mary St. John after she retired in the early 1970s. Today, family members believe Stacy provided John Wayne with camaraderie at a difficult time in his life.

TOP: *Pilar and John Wayne at home in the 1950s.* OPPOSITE, CENTER: *The extended family gathers for a Christmas photo.* OPPOSITE, BOTTOM LEFT: *On a ski trip with their youngest daughter, Marisa.* OPPOSITE, BOTTOM RIGHT: *John Wayne's second family—out on the town with Ethan, Aissa, Pilar, and Marisa (left to right).*

Wayne always strove to keep his family close. He had his brother, Robert Morrison, produce movies for him for many years, until Robert retired from the film business in the mid-1960s. Stories abound of Wayne bringing his brother into the family business at the behest of their mother, Molly, who supposedly insisted that John Wayne "take care" of his younger brother once he became a major Hollywood player. Little can be gleaned about their personal relationship through the letters in the Wayne archives. Robert, who always signed his letters "Brother Bob," wrote entirely about business issues, mainly analyzing or reporting on negotiations or projects in development.

Wayne's children suggest the two brothers drew closer as they got older, and Robert certainly became a beloved uncle to the Wayne children. Robert never had children of his own, and he died of cancer in 1970, soon after their mother passed away.

"Dad and his brother were very close," relates Patrick Wayne. "I knew Uncle Bob very well and saw him daily for many years. He was different than dad—he wasn't as driven to succeed. But he was very bright and witty and strong. He was everything my dad was without quite the same passion to succeed. He was a tremendous guy. He produced for my dad all his working life and then retired, but they were together a long time."

John Wayne likewise kept his two eldest sons close professionally. After a brief acting stint, Wayne's oldest son, Michael, went on to work behind the camera and eventually produced some of his dad's movies and ran his company, Batjac Productions, for many years. His siblings recall Michael would sometimes butt heads with his dad over company business because, as his brother Patrick says, "Michael was his own man and tried to watch out for other things besides just the film production side of things. But in the end, he did what my dad wanted him to do, and he always tried to look out for my dad."

Indeed, Wayne named Michael to serve as an executor of his estate, and after Wayne's death, Michael ran Batjac and John Wayne Enterprises for years. Michael himself passed away in 2003.

Patrick Wayne, now in his seventies, went on to a successful acting career of his own and today runs the John Wayne Cancer Institute. Several letters in the John Wayne archive illustrate his father's unending devotion to Patrick, particularly once he grew up and started going his own way. On October 18, 1977, Wayne wrote his busy son urging him to come for a visit much like any parent would.

"The phone lines are still open to the beach," he wrote. "I live here by myself, have five bedrooms. You could come down and stay overnight if it is too inconvenient to drive this far south;

"DAD AND HIS BROTHER WERE VERY CLOSE," RELATES PATRICK WAYNE.
"I KNEW UNCLE BOB VERY WELL AND SAW HIM DAILY FOR MANY YEARS."

or you could pick up the phone—either of two numbers and say hello."

A couple of years later, on April 29, 1979, just a couple months before his death, John Wayne wrote again simply to tell his son how proud he was of him: "Dear Patrick, My number two son is always a delight to me. Thank you for your continued best efforts. Love, Dad."

By then, of course, Wayne was very sick and realized the end was near. What is striking is how forthright he was over the years when the subject of facing his nemesis—cancer—came up. Wayne spoke of battling the disease with Wayne Warga when Warga traveled to Durango, Mexico, in late March 1969 to research an *Los Angeles Times* article on him.

During the course of their conversation, Wayne described to Warga his reaction in 1964 when doctors first told him he had lung cancer and needed to have his lung removed.

TOP: *Brothers John Wayne and Robert Morrison share a private moment. Robert worked for many years as a producer for Wayne's production companies.* RIGHT: *Wayne with oldest sons Michael (left) and Patrick (right) and wife Pilar.* OPPOSITE: *Three Waynes—Michael, John, and Patrick (left to right) make a grand entrance at the wedding of daughter Toni.*

FAMILY MOMENTS

Warga quoted Wayne as saying, "I sat there, trying to be John Wayne, and gruffly asked, 'You trying to tell me I've got cancer?' Whew, what a shock—and one fist slams into the other. I didn't believe I was dying. Still don't. Luckily, it hadn't spread. After the first operation, I was so swelled I had to lift my own eyelids. I thought I was dying. But people resist death. There's a little pull somewhere in you that begins wanting to stick around a little longer. I felt that pull every time I thought it was over."

Things grew even more serious by the late 1970s—Wayne had heart surgery and soon after learned that he had a new and serious recurrence of cancer. This led to multiple, ultimately fruitless treatments. And yet, outwardly at least, he kept pushing "to stick around a little longer." Only months before his death, for instance, he continued corresponding with author Buddy Atkinson, also a writer/producer on *The Beverly Hillbillies* TV series, about collaborating together on a motion picture based on a novel by Atkinson called *Beau John*. Wayne hoped to star in the

TOP: *At the beach, John Wayne and daughter Aissa make music with conch shells.* OPPOSITE, TOP LEFT: *John and Ethan Wayne enjoying a trip on the* Wild Goose *together.* OPPOSITE, TOP RIGHT: *Offering some driving lessons to a young Ethan Wayne.*

film with Ron Howard, whom he had befriended on *The Shootist* two years earlier. In early 1978, less than a year before Wayne's death, Atkinson wrote Wayne to thank him for, among other things, "cutting through the usual Hollywood crap and taking a personal look" at his novel at a time in his life when he was facing heart surgery.

Wayne's illness prevented him from moving ahead with that project. But it never reduced his interest in family, friends, and his industry. He even put on his game face, donned extra clothing under his tuxedo to mitigate the impact of his startling weight loss, and made a presentation at the 1979 Academy Awards on April 9—his last public appearance—to give out the Best Picture Oscar and declare that he planned "to be around a whole lot longer." His daily schedule for that day says Wayne then enjoyed "a short visit with Cary Grant, Sir Laurence Olivier, and [Lauren] Betty Bacall at the Awards." He then piled into a special motor home and returned briefly to Newport Beach.

On April 13, he entertained guests on the *Wild Goose* and the next day took his final trip to Catalina on the boat. He returned to the hospital on April 18 with a bout of pneumonia,

while the retired Mary St. John briefly returned "to help out," according to the schedule. On April 25, he was discharged from the hospital, and that same day, just six or so weeks before his death, he made a point of sending flowers to his secretarial staff for Secretary's Day.

Wayne returned to the hospital on May 1—the day Ethan Wayne drove him there—and never left. He enjoyed a brief visit from Frank and Barbara Sinatra on May 10, and from that day till the end he visited daily with family. He died at 5:30 p.m. on June 11, 1979, surrounded by his children.

"I got to the hospital real early in the morning," Marisa Wayne remembers. "The doctor came in and told us Dad would probably pass away that morning. He was on morphine and kind of semiconscious, and I remember telling him how much I loved him, and not to worry about me, that I'd be okay. So we did get to say our good-byes. But then he hung on until about five, when he passed.

"His funeral was early in the morning—it was still dark out and was just for family and very close friends at Our Lady Queen of Angels Church in Newport Beach, and then the burial with a view of the Pacific Ocean. At the time, there was no headstone or anything. He finally got one about ten years after he died— my oldest brother, Michael, had been concerned about people

vandalizing the grave because something like that had happened to Charlie Chaplin's grave about a year earlier."

At this writing, Ethan Wayne said the family was mulling over changing the existing marker on Wayne's grave, which features a quote about greeting tomorrow with open arms that John Wayne once offered up to a magazine interviewer. Ethan says the family has been discussing changing his father's tombstone inscription to read simply, "Feo, Furete y Formal"—a Spanish phrase that translates as "ugly, strong, and dignified." Ethan says his father had requested the quote at one point and frequently said he felt the phrase described him.

"That is probably more appropriate," Ethan says in looking back at his father's enormous impact on his life, not to mention millions of others. "It's simpler, and it fits the kind of person he was—he kept things simple and relatable. He was open, accommodating. He'd look you in the eye and tell you yes or no, but he would never hold you up. And he was always trying to move forward. He was kind, positive, and fair. And those are great lessons I got from him—we all got from him. That's the John Wayne I want the world to know." ✪

MEMORIES
OF A
FATHER

Four of John Wayne's five surviving children spoke in highly personal terms about their father in preparation for this book, offering rare anecdotes and insight into their father's world and their relationships with him. Following are a few additional memories they chose to share.

PATRICK WAYNE

ON RAISING TWO FAMILIES:

"It's true that my dad did work more when I was little than when he was raising his second family—he was away more. So my younger brother, Ethan, had a freer hand than we did growing up and he was with him more. By the time my dad had his second family, I was out of the house and had my own family—my sister Marisa and my oldest son are the same age. So by then, Dad and I didn't spend that much time together unless we were working together on a film. But I got time to spend with Ethan, and it developed our relationship. The siblings have always had

great relationships. There is no half brother or half sister thing—no distinctions like that.

"I can remember doing a little Disney niche film [*The Bears and I*] in British Columbia about animals on a very remote, big lake. My dad was going salmon fishing and flew up there on a seaplane with Ethan, who was about ten at the time. My dad told Ethan, 'Why don't you stay with Patrick and I'll pick you up on the way home?' He just took off and left Ethan with me. It was a film about animals, and we had a full zoo there, and I was working around them all the time. Every time I'd turned around, I'd wonder, where is that kid? But it was playful, and we became very close by the time Dad came back. He always worked to make sure we all had great relationships."

ON PURSUING AN ACTING CAREER
AS JOHN WAYNE'S SON:

"The acting thing, when it started, was just me visiting my dad on set. He'd say I could be in the film, and I'd say 'okay.' But as it went on, what happened in the dynamics of the family was that no one else was interested in acting. If I had a chance to act in a film, I'd be the only kid there and not have to compete with siblings for attention. So I jumped at those opportunities.

"And then, separate from my dad, my godfather was John Ford, and he'd tell me, 'We have a part in this picture, do you want to do it?' I got out of school and went to exotic locations, so that was a pretty seductive thing growing up, and eventually, I fell for it.

LEFT: *Taking after their father, brothers Patrick (left) and Michael Wayne (right) enjoy playing cowboy as youngsters.* OPPOSITE, TOP: *John Wayne celebrates with his son Patrick (left) and a friend during a school graduation event.* OPPOSITE, CENTER LEFT: *John Wayne and daughter Melinda on the set of* The Conqueror *in St. George, Utah.* OPPOSITE, BOTTOM LEFT: *Wayne accepts a hug from Melinda.* OPPOSITE, BOTTOM RIGHT: *Melinda and Patrick Wayne as adults.*

"But now, I question whether it was about spending time with my dad and godfather. In any case, I wanted to do it, but my dad never put any pressure on me, although I do think he was happy I did it. It was both a help and a hindrance having John Wayne for a dad if you wanted to act. It did open a lot of doors and I got work that way. But then, if you don't deliver, you won't get hired again. If you don't develop your own niche, then the work stops. The only real piece of advice he ever gave me about acting was to always be prepared and be ready by the time I got to set, and I always tried to do that." ✪

MELINDA WAYNE MUNOZ

ON JOHN WAYNE'S SENSE OF HUMOR:
"One year, I wanted to surprise Patrick and Dad on set while they were making *McLintock!* in Arizona. When I arrived, I went to the wardrobe mistress to see if I could get into costume and fool them. She dressed me in an Indian costume. After the

scene [was shot], I stood in line with all of the other actresses [in Native American costume], waiting to get John Wayne's autograph. I just joined the extras and others waiting for a chance to get him to sign his name. He signed for each person, including me, while appearing not to recognize me. After he signed them all, I looked at what he wrote for me, and it read, "Hi Melinda, when did you get here?"

I later asked him, "How did you know it was me?" He said, "Your smile gave you away."

ON NAMING HER DAUGHTER
WITH HER FATHER'S HELP:

"We lost my grandmother in 1970, and my twins were born soon after. A few weeks after my grandmother died, my father came to see the babies—a boy and a girl. He asked what I was going to call the girl. She was small—only about three pounds, much smaller than her brother. My father said she looked like his mother, my grandmother, whom he always called Molly Brown because her name was Molly. I said, 'That's a great name,' and we called my daughter Molly. I always tell her that her grandfather, John Wayne, named her." ✪

ON JOHN WAYNE'S FORD F250 PICKUP TRUCK, WHICH REMAINS IN THE FAMILY:

"My dad's partner at the 26 Bar Ranch, Louis Johnson, said to him one day that he would get four bales of cotton per acre [during harvest] or he would buy my dad a new truck. If he did get the four bales, my dad had to buy him a new Cadillac. That first year, Dad was right and Louis Johnson bought the pickup truck for him. Every other year, my dad was buying him Cadillacs. The truck has now been in the family since 1968—my brother Patrick had it for a while. I've since restored it twice over the past twenty-five years."

ON LIVING WITH JOHN WAYNE IN NEWPORT BEACH AS A CHILD:

"I remember just following my father everywhere. I just wanted to be with him all the time. At night, we would lie down on the bed, and I would fall asleep talking to him. I'd hear him talk to the TV, commenting about Nixon or Vietnam or whatever. He would talk to the TV if something important were in the news.

"I loved the big den. It was sort of a big rectangle. One wall was all sliding glass doors that faced the yard, and the other wall was a fireplace in the center with two banks of cabinets that were very high with drawers. Then, there were gun racks for his rifles and other things. There was a ledge along the top, just barely down below the ceiling, and that is where he had his kachina dolls lined up. There was also a bookshelf with projectors going through it, and at the other end was an alcove with a desk. A screen would come down in front of that desk; we would turn the couch around to have two big couches facing the big screen. We screened movies there constantly—the studios would send him prints to watch."

ON ATTENDING THE 1970 OSCARS AS AN EIGHT-YEAR-OLD CHILD:

"I definitely remember Oscar night when Dad won his award for *True Grit*. They told me to put on a suit, and I felt it was uncomfortable. Then, we go to the event and there came all these lights and the big crowd. At one point, while talking to people, he handed me the award, but I didn't really know what it was. If you see pictures from that night, he'd be talking to someone and I'd be holding the Oscar like a rifle, kind of pointing it around and playing with it." ✪

BELOW: *Ethan Wayne dresses the part on the set of* The Green Berets.
RIGHT: *Ethan Wayne at the 1970 Academy Awards.*

ON A GOLFING OUTING WITH HER DAD:
"While he was shooting *Rooster Cogburn*, my dad had a day off and took me golfing at a resort in Oregon. He said, 'Let's go hit some balls'—Ethan, my dad, and I. But I couldn't hit the ball, so my dad came around and tried to teach me. I swung and missed the ball entirely. When I turned around, I had completely knocked out my father—I had hit him with the club, and he had blood on his head.

"They got him to the hospital and he was fine. But it was in the temple and could have been much worse. He had a dent in his head for the rest of his life from it. My brothers and sisters jokingly sent me a telegram thanking me for 'doing what we wanted to do for years.' I thought he was going to kill me, but he was really sweet about it. But he did go from calling me 'princess' to calling me 'nine iron' after that. It was the same eye where he wore his eye patch in the movie, and they actually had to make the patch bigger to cover the wound for the rest of the shoot."

ON JOHN WAYNE'S SECRET CANDY STASH:
"In the den where the screening room was is where all his awards were, and that is also where he kept his candy. I remember looking for a pen one day and opening up a cabinet and seeing boxes and boxes of Tootsie Rolls and Abba-Zabas. This was his own private little stash, and he never told us about it. He had a real sweet tooth and loved Tootsie Rolls and Abba-Zabas." ✪

LEFT: *Ethan, John, and Marisa Wayne.* BELOW: *John Wayne with his youngest daughter Marisa.*

ACKNOWLEDGMENTS

THE AUTHOR WOULD LIKE TO OFFER PROFOUND GRATITUDE TO ETHAN WAYNE for making this entire endeavor possible and allowing me get to know his late father as the man he was beyond the stereotypical icon I and millions of others grew up with. Ethan let me have unfettered access to the John Wayne archive, where I spent many days studying the personal impact Duke had on those who knew him best, while learning how he lived, loved, worked, and communicated. Ethan also boldly decided this should be an intimately personal book designed to show the world the authentic John Wayne. Along those lines, he introduced me to his family members, whom I would also like to thank for sharing their insight and memories—much gratitude to Patrick, Melinda, Marisa, and Pilar for all their help.

Ethan also graciously allowed his team at John Wayne Enterprises to devote far more time to this project than we had any right to expect. Indeed, this book could never have come to a successful conclusion without their efforts, particularly those of Amy Shepherd, Katrina Seidel, Jonathan Dupree, and Elisabeth Morris. Amy and Katrina were tireless and cheerful partners and dedicated professionals throughout this process.

On the publishing side, deep gratitude to Insight Editions' publisher Raoul Goff and editor Steve Korte for bringing me into this project. Thanks also to acquisitions editor Robbie Schmidt and associate editor/project manager Becky Duffett. Becky was a calm, clear-thinking editor and sounding board, and a pleasure to work with.

I would also like to thank someone I never met—the late journalist/author Wayne Warga. Decades ago, Warga enthusiastically pursued John Wayne and pressed him to put his life story down on paper. Although that effort never finished, Warga left behind a treasure trove of material that was priceless in informing the direction of portions of this book.

Thanks also to my attorney, Yonatan Hagos, and business manager, Sue Richman.

As always, great appreciation and love go out to my wife, Bari, and my two boys, Jake and Nathan. And finally, I would like to dedicate my success on this project to my mother, Lynn Einstein, my earliest and most unflinching supporter. She and my stepfather, Lionel Groberman, provided unending assistance throughout this effort.

—MICHAEL GOLDMAN

PHOTO CREDITS

The publisher would like to thank John Wayne Enterprises, custodian of the John Wayne Archives, for providing unfettered access to their private and personal collection. Best efforts were made by the publisher to find and credit the photographers. The publisher makes no specific claim of ownership of images contained in this book and is claiming no specific copyright to images used.

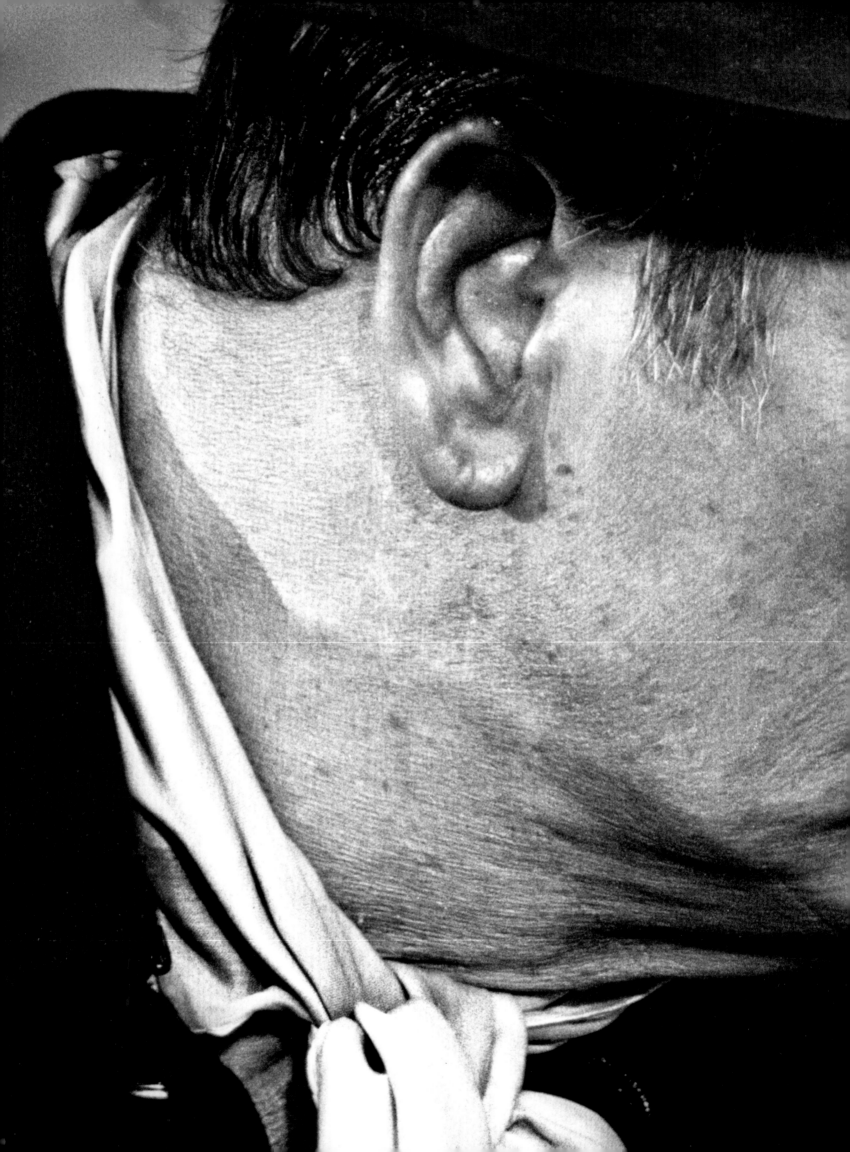

ABOUT THE AUTHOR

Michael Goldman is a veteran entertainment-industry journalist and author. He has edited for *Daily Variety* and *Millimeter* magazines, and contributes regularly to *American Cinematographer*. He has written six books, including *Clint Eastwood: Master Filmmaker at Work*. He lives in Los Angeles with his wife and two sons.

ETHAN WAYNE

Ethan Wayne, John Wayne's youngest son, is currently president of John Wayne Enterprises, the sole and exclusive steward of the John Wayne brand. In addition, Ethan also serves as director of John Wayne Cancer Foundation (JWCF), a nonprofit organization established by the Wayne family following John Wayne's own heroic battle with cancer. Since its founding in 1985, the JWCF has supported research, education programs, awareness programs, and support programs in its mission to bring courage, strength, and grit to the fight against cancer.

PRESIDENT JIMMY CARTER

Jimmy Carter was the thirty-ninth president of the United States (1977–81) and received the 2002 Nobel Peace Prize. Both in and out of office, he has been a peacemaker and champion of human rights. For thirty years, his nonprofit Carter Center has worked to wage peace, fight disease, and build hope in poor nations.

INSIGHT ◉ EDITIONS

PO Box 3088
San Rafael, CA 94912
www.insighteditions.com

Find us on Facebook: www.facebook.com/InsightEditions
Follow us on Twitter: @insighteditions

Publisher: Raoul Goff
Co-publisher: Michael Madden
Associate Publisher: Sharon Donovan
Art Director: Chrissy Kwasnik
Designer: Michel Vrana
Production Managers: Jane Chinn, Anna Wan
Acquisitions Editor: Robbie Schmidt
Associate Editor: Becky Duffett
Editorial Assistant: Leigh Mitnick

ISBN: 978-1-60887-116-2

ROOTS of PEACE ◉ REPLANTED PAPER

Insight Editions, in association with Roots of Peace, will plant two trees for each tree used in the manufacturing of this book. Roots of Peace is an internationally renowned humanitarian organization dedicated to eradicating land mines worldwide and converting war-torn lands into productive farms and wildlife habitats. Roots of Peace will plant two million fruit and nut trees in Afghanistan and provide farmers there with the skills and support necessary for sustainable land use.

Manufactured in China by Insight Editions

10 9 8 7 6 5 4 3 2 1

Insight Editions wishes to thank the following people for their generous support in producing this book: Jeff Campbell, Jon Glick, Jody Revenson, Andrea Santoro, and Rich Wright. Many thanks to John Wayne Enterprises, especially Jonathan Dupree, Katrina Seidel, Amy Shepherd, and Ethan Wayne.